GRANDMA SAYS:
WAKE UP,
WORLD!

TAOWHYWEE,
AGNES BAKER
PILGRIM

Transcribed and edited from
the audiobook of the same name

Printed in the United States of America

First Printing, 2015

ISBN 978-1-5046-8691-4

Blackstone Publishing
31 Mistletoe Rd.
Ashland, OR 97520

www.Downpour.com

CONTENTS

1
INTRODUCTION

My name is Agnes Pilgrim. My native name is Taowhywee. My father's name was George Baker, and my mother's name was Evelynn Lydia Harney-Baker. My mother was the daughter of Chief George Harney, the first elected chief of the Confederated Tribes of Siletz. There was nine of us children, and I was the third from the end. I am the only one left of all of us. My grandmother is gone. My grandfathers, my aunts, uncles, all my brothers and sisters have gone, and I am the oldest living now of the Takelma Indians that lived in Southern Oregon for 22,000 years. I am sitting in a studio here in Ashland, Oregon, trying to put words together that can help anyone, whether it's a child or whether it is an elder or a great-great-great-great-grandma or great-great-great-great grandfather. I pray that the words that I will leave when I go to the Star Nation will help somebody, that they have choices.

Whatever you do, think of the consequences. I don't want you to forget that you always have a choice no matter what your age is. It's called *life*. That was the greatest gift our Creator gave us. The next thing He gave us was this thinkin' thing called your brain. It is up to you how you run it. It is put on the top of your body to run the rest of your body. It will tell you about your choices. Is it good for you, what you're choosing? Nobody is going to tell you not to do it, and if they do, you have a right to say, "I know the consequences."

Here I am at ninety years old. What would you think of me if I was pouring alcohol down, or drugs, or sitting here smoking a cigarette? I don't think it would be me sittin' here. I think I would have been long gone, but I pray that whoever gets these words and hears me, don't forget you have a choice. Just one day at a time. That's all life anywhere can do, one day at a time. You can do it. Be big about it. Be grateful. Be grateful just for life that you can do this for yourself.

Think logically. I pray that you can make a difference with your body by how you run your brain. It's the longest journey any of us can make—it's, I say, fourteen inches from your brain to your heart. When you get to your heart, I call it the "ah ha" stage. *Ah ha*, now I know who I am. *Ah ha*, now I know where I am goin'. *Ah ha*, now I know what I am supposed to be doin'. I pray that you will get to that journey. I pray that you use that thinkin' thing to think about all this and make a good choice. A lot of people will love you for that. You'll have better friends, nicer friends, get along better with everybody, 'cause with it will come kindness. When you've got kindness you want kindness. People will treat you with kindness. If you have kindness, if you have compassion for your life, they will give it back to you.

I pray that someday, if I am still on this planet, you will come to me and say, "I did it, Grandma. I made a good choice." And I pray that I will hear some of these voices and see some of you that have made that choice. Don't go down that awful, awful road. Stay on the Red Road. Come along with me. Thank you.

2
THE STORY OF MY PEOPLE

I remember how hard it was when I was a child growing up because in those times, in Lincoln County, there was signs on restaurants and different places where Indians and dogs weren't allowed. And you know, I grew up from that era, but I am not bitter about it. What was is what was. I know I am limited. I can only change right now. I can't change anything a minute ago, an hour ago, a day ago, a week ago, or a year ago, so I know I am limited. So, what I did was I forgave all of that in my background, of what happened to our people. The Trail of Tears that started here in Southern Oregon in 1856. They were all gathered up here, then run north. They lived here for over 22,000 years, and they actually felt that the Creator had given them this land, it was theirs eternally, forever and forever, as long as the grass grew and the water flowed. It was a hard time for my people in those times, you know, going up in rough terrain in inclement weather. They were force-marched in stormy weather with just moccasins on their feet. They could take one thing, and most of them just carried food wrapped in what they could carry. So then their moccasins wore out, and the elders fell along the wayside. The young were taught to take care of the elders, so they would run back and pick them up, and they were beaten. The guards told them that if they did that again they'd just leave the elders by the wayside for the animals to eat.

It was a terrible time for them, over two hundred miles of this land going north and to trails where there was no trails. I can fathom how hard it was. And then, after all that journey, when they did get up to Siletz, the agent had used up a lot of the money, so there wasn't enough blankets to go around. There wasn't enough food, and many of them perished. It was awful. It's a wonder I sit here. But it was all different, you know? With all the Indians together, many of them had to learn the sign language of the Chinook Jargon to communicate. So, it was a terrible time. Before they had to leave, they had their sweat lodges and ritualistically believed in taking sweats and doing the sweat lodges because it was such a spiritual thing. Then they didn't have that. Many of them said they couldn't wear any of their regalia because they didn't want the law at that time—they didn't want an uprising. They didn't want fighting. When they ran out of food, they had no weapon to go hunt for anything because government took away everything. They just went with the clothes on their backs to a land where they didn't know which way to go to get anything to eat. Then my grandfather, Chief George Harney, walked clear across the mountain, clear over there to the Grand Ronde. He helped them over there and worked with the people over there to the point where they had his big, long picture inside of the Catholic church in Old Town in honor to Chief George Harney for helping the Grand Ronde Indians.

The government from the White House said, "You Indian people, we cannot help to fund you for housing and health and education and things. You're going to have to be more self-sustaining." So Vine Deloria, the Congress of American Indians, Ben Campbell, a lot of the political Indian people that were at that time invisible, they came together because the government said they had to do something. So the Indians got together and thought, you know, we have the land; if we could just build something on it.

In all of the tribal people, there wasn't televisions and radios and things for entertainment. They had card games and stick games and bone games for entertainment. After the war, the

Spanish left some horses. Some of the Indians, like in Klamath Falls and Chinook, began to have horse races for entertainment and being competitive and creating fun to come together. So the Congress of American Indians and all of these high people in politics said that the Indians have land and they already were gamblers, so they could put a casino up and raise money for their housing and education and such things. That's how, through coercion, came the casinos, because they said that we had to be more self-sustaining.

3
CHILDHOOD

Way back then, it was just a way of life: we grew everything we needed. We had gardens of all kinds of vegetables. We had apple orchards and pears and cherries, and my dad made nets, built boats, taught my brothers how to go hunting. They had trap lines. Right now I could take you to the trap lines that my brothers used, coming back with their mink or their otter or something from the trap. In the springtime they would have in their arms the bleeding hearts and the trilliums, the dogwood flowers, and an armload of these flowers for my mom because she was ailing in her health, and they would bring her all these flowers. They would come and put them in a big bucket, all these flowers, and they were all in the house, which was just really great at those times, and Mom just loved it. I always think of my brothers, you know, how good of guys they were, even when they were young, to do that for Mom and take time out to pick all these things for her. The flowers were all over, across the river and under the trees, and they would go along and take time out to pick these flowers for my mom.

When I was three years old my dad plowed the ground all up and had it all fixed and planted. I was taught to have four plants. They took me out there and showed me the difference between a weed and a plant. I had to keep the weeds out of the plants. Dad took the label off a big tomato can and drilled some holes and put a wire bale over the top for a handle. I had to go clear down to the creek, fill it up, and water my poor little plants every day. Pretty soon, as I got older, so did the plants get longer. Then it was time to go to school, and pretty soon I had about four big, long rows I had to take care of either before I went to school or when I came home. So did my brothers. They had cows to milk. They had sheep to tend to. We had longhorn cattle. We had horses, and we had all of these things that my brothers had to learn how to take care of. We had to feed the chickens and clean the chicken pen up, gather the eggs. We had our chores from the time that we were just little kids. When the beans grew—we had what we called the bush bean—we had to go out there and pick them, and we put them in a gunnysack. When the gunnysack was full we tied a string around the top, and then we would lay it out close to the house, and we would jump up and down on it to knock all the beans out. Mom would take all the beans, and she would wash them up, and then she would can them. They were the best-tasting beans; I wish we could do that again.

We had to take care of the garden with rutabagas, corn, rhubarb, berries, and loganberries and raspberry bushes. And we had to take care of all these things all the time; even when we went to school, we had our chores. We weren't lazy kids. We weren't allowed to be. We had to come home from school and do these things before the sun went down, plus our homework. So, we were kids that were taught not to be fighting around with each other and how to behave, and when to keep your mouth shut, like when the 111s came into our room, us kids immediately knew we had to shut up and be quiet because that was the medicine people coming in.

We were taught respect even when someone passed away and it wasn't a relative. One of my brothers or my dad would lift us up to look into the casket at that person lying there because they said someday one of them would leave us and we would have to know how to deal with loss. We experienced that. There was life, and there was also death and the meaning of it. They taught us this even if that person in the casket wasn't a relative that we knew; but they did, the older ones did. So, we were taught how to deal with loss. I am thankful to this day that I teach the same thing to my children. They were good teachers.

How do you use your time? There's a time to romp and have fun. My brother and my cousin and his sister, my cousin Ida, we had gunnysacks, and a mile from our house up a mountain there was a huge apple orchard—they called it Red Ant Hill. We decided we'd go up there and get some different kind of apples. Off we went, and we went up this mountain and we got our apples and we come back. Well, my dad got home and he saw that. He said, "Where did these come from?" So we told him. "Out to the woodshed you go." We were shaken up. We knew we were gonna get whipped. He whipped us because, he said, "That's stealing, and you are never to take anything that doesn't belong to you." "Nobody lives up there, Dad." We were crying and trying to explain, "Nobody lives up there and they got apples that we don't have." "I don't care. That's stealing. And don't you ever do that again. Don't ever take anything that does not belong to you. Never, or you know you are gonna get it." He even told us if we got in trouble at school, we'd get it when we got home. So we behaved ourselves. We learned not to take anything that didn't belong to us. We didn't take anything from each other that way. It was a good teaching. It was a hard way to teach us, but we learned quick so that we wouldn't get whipped again.

My mother was very concerned about us kids. She taught us cleanliness, how to wash and bathe ourselves so we could do it by ourselves. We were taught how to eat with manners. My dad said that when we all sat down and my mother said the blessings, our table was not a war zone. If we had any differences with each other, we couldn't be doing it at the table, that's not the place to be carrying on your arguments. We were taught that. Grandmother taught us that prayer was a great thing, and we all learned to do that when we were young.

I had to learn to wash on a washboard. My brother said, "If you want to go with us, then you got to do my shirts." So I had to do their shirts up. We made our own starch. I mixed flour and water and made starch to starch their shirts. We had these sad-irons that would sit on the back of the stove. We had a kitchen range that had little shelves above, which I don't see anymore, and a water reservoir on the side. Then on one side was a great big thing, like a griddle. We always had hot water there.

When we were going to school, my uncles would come down and visit with Mom. One of my uncles would put beans on the stove; he could sure make good beans. They'd cook all day for us. I had to learn to cook when I was just a kid. My sisters said, "Someday you kids will grow up and be married. You've got to learn all these things." When we washed the dishes, they even checked us that we were doing it right. Did we scald them right? Did we get them clean and everything? Mom would see that we checked out. Whatever we did, we better do it right or we had to do it over.

We got good instructions. When the elders would come my dad would say, "Okay, you kids, you have made your noise romping around all day, and now we've got company. You're going to have to sit and be quiet. So get you a book. Get your tablet and pencil if you want to do something, and be quiet and get over there." Sometimes we would play cribbage. My dad had a deck of cards. He would take all the face cards out, and he'd have a list on a paper—what kind of numbers would make four, five, six, and all these numbers, out of the rest of the cards. We had to learn addition and subtraction from these cards. He'd call out numbers to us, and multiplication and division, so we learned to do those things with a deck of cards that all the face cards were taken out of because we didn't have television and we didn't have other things. We had to make our own entertainment.

My dad was a musician, so we had to learn music. He could play violin, piano, and guitar. He said, "You kids are going to have to learn some music here because life is a beautiful thing if you can put some music to it." It would make us fit and belong anywhere we went. We all had to learn, so eventually we had our own band. We played for dances and stuff, sing in different bands, and I played my guitar and played the piano in school with everybody dancing or singing around. There's still a couple of older ones in my tribe that remember me doing this in high school. We learned that music was a very crucial thing for our lives. My brothers, they had to learn the violin and guitar and everything, too. When we did, we found out my dad's words were true. It really made us to fit in and feel we belonged when I used to play in high school.

Even though I grew up where there was signs in the stores and restaurants and places where Indians and dogs weren't allowed, I was already proud of who I was as a young girl because I knew my grandfather was the chief of our tribe. Although he was gone in 1912, I knew about him, and I thought how proud it made all of us kids to know about him. So I grew up with that honorable feeling because . . . those signs of Indians and dogs not allowed in places, it really . . . I didn't like it, but it didn't affect me, is what I'm saying. I was proud of who I was as a descendent of Chief George Harney. That was royalty to me, in my tribe. In my way of thinking, I was following royalty.

My brothers learned to shoot archery, and I had to learn to shoot a .22 rifle and a .30-06 and a 9mm Luger that I used to strap on my hip. When I would go out into the woods to get berries or whatever I had it on me, but I had to learn to shoot it. I was a pretty good shot. So, we were taught a lot of things.

My dad would build our boats for the boys, and he made nets. They built a big platform by the creek that we would dam up, and they would put the salmon in the creek. They'd gut them, and we'd have to jump in the creek and wash the fish all out and throw them up on this wooden table that they built. We were busy doing all these things.

My dad had a tomato can that he drilled a hole in and put a bale on it. We'd shimmy up these trees, put two or three apples in the can, let it down. Our mom would be sitting by the sled where all the boxes were filled with straw, and she would take the apples out of our cans to put them in these boxes. When it was all full, the horse would pull it all to the house. Dad built a cellar down in the ground, all tapered. It wasn't all flat. He would line it with straw, and we'd have to put all these apples on this straw that we had. During Halloween we'd go down and get some apples to put at our door for those people that would come, and oh! when we opened that cellar door the aroma was so great. It would smell so good with all the apples we had in it.

We had to gather eggs; we had a lot of chickens. At lambing time we had to sit and hold the lambs' tails that my brothers would chop off, and blood would splatter all over us kids. Dad would have some turpentine in a bucket there and put turpentine on their tails. The poor little lambs would go crying and running. They sheered the sheep and sold the wool. We had that to do, too.

The life that I look back on, we were never hungry. There was constant things from season to season, whether it was berry time—Mom made candy, we had hot chocolate and tea. She cooked for the harvesters. They would go and each help each other, and she would be one of the cooks. She was such a great cook. She had the best pie crust, everybody said. My dad would go get one deer a year and render it out, and us girls would have to watch the fat in the oven in a big roasting pan till it got all the fat cooked out. We would get our lard in these big wooden kegs, so when one was empty, my dad would use that to put salt and salmon in it or whatever we had. We had our chores to do with all that, too, learning how to wash jars and help my mom. We had to learn how to peel apples and pears, and we cut up potatoes when she canned and put the potatoes in with the deer meat and the onions, and we had to help with all of that.

So, us girls grew up good cooks, and I am proud to say that if I have to cook a meal today, I could do it, but my daughter does it all now. Us girls, my sisters, were all wonderful cooks. We even saved the apple skins from the apples that my mother would cook and strain, and we'd make jelly. We had all kinds of jellies. Our pantry was always full because Mom was canning something all the time. We had to learn how to run the smokehouse as we got bigger, and how to strip the fish and put them on the racks, how to keep the fire and how hot to keep it. We were busy from one season to the next season gathering our food, canning. We had to know how many hours to cook the fish on the stove in the big—I remember it was a big blue granite pot—three hours to keep it boiling to cook the fish.

My mother and brothers would get deer meat, and we'd cut it all up in pieces, roll it in flour and brown it, poke it in these jars and can all of it so that when Mom took it out, she could make soup, or she could make gravy—just add water and stir it up. It was so good with all our food. It makes me hungry right now thinkin' about it. My brothers had to go gather the cows and to milk them. My cousin and one of my brothers one time went and found the cows, and they had cow bells on them, and they stuffed moss up in there so the little bell thing wouldn't ring. When Dad came home he said, "Did you milk the cows?" And my brother— he was young—he says, "Couldn't find 'em, Dad." So, Dad lit the lanterns and out they went lookin' for the cows, and boy, the boys got a whippin' when he found them with the moss in the bells so they wouldn't ring. Crazy things like that, they done. Dad had to stop them one time, too, because during the summertime, when the berry bushes were gettin' kind of dry from the sun, they'd go put 'em on fire so the rabbits would run out so that they could shoot them. Dad had to put a stop to them doing that.

My mother loved horses, and she could trade horses and break horses. Where men would beat on horses and everything, she would just walk around them and whistle and talk to them and pat them. To be able to break horses—where men couldn't break these horses, she did. And she could whistle. She had the most beautiful whistle; she could whistle all kinds of these old songs. She whistled around the horses, and whenever she wanted them she whistled and here they'd come. One of the horses that they called Old Chip, they taught him to put his head down so—all of us kids were little then—one of us would get on his neck, and he'd raise up his head and we'd slide down on his back. Then he'd put his head back down for the next kid, until four of us got on his back like that, and he would haul us around, and when we wanted off he would stop. He would always do, we didn't have to say. When we got back to the barn, he would put his head down, and we'd slide off, all four, one at a time. But that was a great horse that my mom taught to be that way for us kids. Old Chip was quite a horse for us kids to take out and ride around with.

When I was just a kid—eight, nine years old—my mother was bedridden, but there I was, just a child, standing on an apple box cooking for my mom. She would tell me what to do. It was hard because we had lamps and lanterns, no electricity. Had to get our water from the spring, heat the water in a big copper boiler on top of the stove, wash clothes on a washboard. Then my mother was getting worse, and my other two sisters had left and gone on and was working away from home, so I became the little mother. I had to learn to cook when I was nine years old, standing on an apple box, with my mom giving me instructions from her bed. When I went to school and somebody had to come and take care of Mom while I was at school, then my Aunt Agnes would come down to stay with Mom till I got home. Used to take me up in the sweat lodge when I was just a little kid. We had one by the creek, and she used to call me Susan Applesauce because I always loved applesauce. My grandma would come and, "Come on, Susan Applesauce." She would take me by the hand, and we'd walk up through the woods; about a mile from our house is where she lived.

My grandfather fought hard for allotments, so my aunts all got allotments, eighty acres. Mom let my grandma live up there by the creek where she had water and they could pump it up to her house. And up in the woods, they built her a big house up there. She'd come and get me. "You need a break. Come on." My uncles called me Samantha Ann. They'd take me up there, and Uncle would be having the fire going by the sweat house, and Grandma would put me in it and take the little dome thing and put it over us. She'd have the water bucket in a bush of huckleberries and dip it in there and sprinkle it on the rocks. The first time I went in there, this bird came through. "What was that bird, Gram? It just flew right in here!" She never did tell me, but that was the eagle—Spirit Eagle—that came. A long time after, she told me that's what it was and that I was blessed. You know? And she was blessed for bringing me in there because the eagle come floppity, swings inside the tiny sweat lodge. It had to be Spirit inside that little thing. Anyways, she'd periodically take me up there to the sweat lodge, and we would sit on Mother Earth and look up, and she said, "Look, above your head is the Creator," and we would sit on the Mother Earth, and the fire there in the pit would touch the fire inside of us. And that warmth would always be with us. She said how the water would bless our bodies, and we had all these pores that needed to breathe and to be touched by the heat in the sweat and how it purifies your mind and lifts you up, elevates you closer to the Creator.

It was something to experience way back then when I was a kid. I was kind of scared at first, but with Gram there, I didn't think nothing much would happen with her by me, so I would go along with her. My uncles, they'd spend a lot of time with us and come down, and we'd be cookin' and havin' stew or beans, or somethin' cookin' slowly all day on the stove, playing solitaire. They lived at our house a lot. Everybody came, but you know, if you came to my house and you just got through eatin', you didn't say you'd already ate. You didn't dare say that. You'd eat again. I've done that all my life. I've gone to someone's house, you sit down, you eat. You don't say, "I already ate." You don't do that. You sit down and you eat something.

My mother, when she was ill, made my brother Tiny—his name was Lloyd Harney, he's named after Chief George Harney: Lloyd Harney Baker. We called him Tiny, but he never was tiny. He was a fat little guy, and he grew up a big guy, but anyway, she would make Tiny sit down beside her, and she said, "I don't want Agnes and kids going to Samoa Indian School, because all they teach 'em is how to smoke and drink." He promised Mom that when she left, he wouldn't send us two youngest kids out there. She wanted us to go to a "regular school," she said, meaning that we would go to schools right around where we lived and go on the bus. So, he promised.

When she did go, they didn't send us out there, although I'd been back and forth out to Chemawa Indian School, so that's why I went to the Lincoln School, a one-room little schoolhouse. Anyway, I kept on like that. I was going to sleep in class, and finally the principal found out why I was sleeping in class— because I was waking up at night. My mom had a big long stick, and I had my bed close to her, and she would poke me with that stick when she had to have her medications. I would get up in the night and give her her medication. Get her her water and let her go to the bathroom and all of that, and take care of her. So I was getting sleepy in school. Then the principal of Lincoln County put all my classes in the morning, and the teachers let me sleep in the teachers' room after my lunch. I would sleep until four o'clock, when they'd wake me up and I would catch the bus and go home.

I didn't know at the time that my mom was slowly going to leave me. When she did, we sent word down to another Indian lady, Pearl Relatos, who lived by the store in Logsden. I called her Mother Pearl. Mother Pearl came when my mother went on and helped me to bathe my mom. I had a bandage that I used to tied her ankles, and I tied her knees, crossed her arms over and put the bandage around, because somehow or another I thought that if she got stiff and they had to break my mom's arms or legs, I couldn't handle that. So I tied them up. Mother Pearl said, "That's okay. You can do that," 'cause I was only twelve years old. I was crying and trying to fix my mom, bathe her, wash her up and dress her and put her in a new nightgown. When the hearse came and got her, we followed it into Toledo, Oregon, and we had her nice clothes. We dressed her there in the mortuary, and it was a hard time for me.

Mother Pearl's husband drove the school bus, and when Mom was gone, if he didn't see any smoke coming out of our chimney when he came by, he'd come and wake me up, and then he'd go on up the line and pick up the students up there and then come on back down, and we'd be dressed and ready and jump in the bus. We'd go clear down to Logsden Store to his house, because they lived right close there, by that covered bridge. Mother Pearl would have breakfast for us, and then we'd wait for the school bus coming from up Nashville way to pick us up and take us down into Siletz, because I was the only one at home anymore.

My other brothers were in logging camps, and my dad was out working and wouldn't come home till Friday, so I had my little brother to take care of. I had a shotgun at one door and a .22 at the other and a mean dog, so we were way out in the country and nobody bothered us. Even my cousins—they'd come, they'd holler way out there to let us know they'd come up to check on us, because they didn't want to get bit. Mother Pearl and her husband were really good to me when I was taking care of my mom, and they always treated me as family. I always say we're all connected, anyway.

Then, after Mother Pearl went on, my brother and his wife took care of me. I stayed with them and moved down out of Gleneden Beach with them. I had to get a bus to go to school in Taft, which is called Lincoln City now. Even though I grew up where the signs said "No Dogs and Indians Allowed," it didn't make me bitter, didn't make me hate the white race. When my mom and dad left and went up there, my brothers said, "We can't take care of you girls, so you got to learn to box." So they taught us how to box. "Watch my hand! Look at my footwork. Hit my hand! Hit my hand!" They made boxers out of us, so nobody messed with us.

Most everybody around where I grew up didn't bother me. I was always for the underdog. I didn't like nobody bein' picked on, whether they were black, green, or white, you know? There were some girls from Switzerland that, every time I got in the bus—if I wasn't there, the kids picked on them—I would duke it out with those who picked on those Swiss girls. So, they stopped. I was a fair person. I wanted everybody to be treated fairly.

Then my sister got sick, and I had to quit my job in Tillamook and had to go to Crescent City, California, to take care of her.

When I get down there, I go downtown, and there's some young women that thought they couldn't whup my sister, but one of 'em's kid sister said, "We'll duke it out with her. We'll fix her up." Well, they didn't get to do that. They got the dirty end of it. Of all things, I kicked off my high-heeled shoes, and I am out there on the sidewalk, and one walked out in the street and grabbed the other one by a handful of hair and flipped her on top of the other one out in the street. The other one gets up and comes at me, and I knocked her back and knocked the other one down again. By that time there is an officer here on my shoulder: "What's goin' on?" I looked up; it was the chief of police, who was part Cherokee Indian. I said, "Nothing now."

When I graduated from there in 1940, there was only two Indians, a young boy and me. Only two Indians in that school. At the time that I had to give my valedictorian speech I was crying because my mother always kept telling me, "You go on and get that piece of paper, Sissy, 'cause you'll be proud that you do. You get your education. It's going to be important; if you want to get good money someday, then you better get that piece of paper, that diploma." So I always heard my mother's voice in the wind, "You keep on studying. You keep on studying. You keep on studying so you can get that piece of paper called a diploma, so you can get a good job someday. And you keep on studying." I promised my mom I would do that, and I have.

When I was standing up there giving my speech at graduation day, I was just crying, saying, "These words are for you, Mom. I got my piece of paper, and I will go on to get an education like I promised you." And right now, thinkin' about all this I have—I went back to college when I was fifty years old. I got my associate of arts at College of the Redwoods, and I got my BA degree at Southern Oregon University in Native American studies. I accomplished what my mother wanted me to do. I wanted my PhD, but I got cancer and I couldn't do it. I said, "Well, maybe that is just PhD—stands for Piled High and Deep." I said I have it piled high and deep, anyway. I feel good that I did all these things, 'cause my mom, I could hear her voice in the wind: "You keep on, Sister. You can do it. You can do it. You can do it." That encouragement would always come to me across the veil from my mom. So, I am feeling good about bringing her into this story today, because she knows I'm tellin' the truth about it all. How I kept hearing her say, "You can do it. You can do it."

I am glad that I went on to college, and I still study. I still do a lot of stuff and research, and if I have things that I must learn—if I find a word that I don't know the meaning of—I have all sizes of dictionaries in my house, so I am always looking up words that I don't know. I am still studying. I always tell my mom, "I am still hanging in there."

All of these things concerning my mom and my gran, my uncles, and all of them, it took all of them to make these balance in all of us kids. We had our hands into everything from the time we were little to when we grew up. We had to help do; we had to help each other. It was a hard time. But I don't remember being angry about anything I had to do. I became a little momma to everybody, I guess, in those days. I still got that way when I grew up and came back; anything happened to my brothers and sisters, they'd call me. I would drop whatever I was doin' and go and help. And I am glad that I can say that now, because when I think of them, I think of them with love. I loved them all and I miss them so greatly, so many times. I think of their funny words and their jolliness, and I pray that I'm doing okay in their sight, too.

4

BEING AN ELDER

I am very proud to be able to live this long because I think that as an elder and a grandmother, it's important how you lead your family. As a grandmother, I feel like I am the glue to my family. I am the glue to my community. I am the glue to my tribe. It's very important, I think, that elders look at how they are leading their family. When you leave this world, do you leave a good legacy for your children? I have been talking to many, many elders: stop the alcohol, stop the drugs, stop the tobacco and all these things that are shortening your life. If the Creator wanted these things in our bodies, we would have been created with them in it. I chose not to use any of those things, and I teach that. As elders, we need to be able to say we can walk our talk. Because when you got one foot in this world and one in the other, you better watch what you're doin'. If you believe there's a heaven and you want to get there, think about it. As an elder of my tribe, I still go to a committee up there, a culture committee and sacred lands, because I believe our culture and traditions are the glue to our tribe and it's very important.

A long time ago I was a young mother. I came to my tribe in a white buckskin dress. Some of the women elders said, "You've already had children. You can't wear white." I said, "Listen, the way I look at what I got on, I have earned it." And so from that, a lot of the men—some of them are going on now—our tribe knows those men supported me and said, "Yes. She has earned it." So they accepted that, that I have earned it. Then a lot of our Indian women elders began to come to our gatherings in white buckskin, and I feel so happy about that because they have earned theirs, too.

And another thing: it's not us adults that own this world, it's the children. Remember that, you elders. And think about it; it's the children that own the world. I pray that I work hard so that for the next seven generations, the unborn, when they come, there will be good water and good air for them. It should be your job, too, to be that voice and look after the green of our Mother Earth. Today I feel that the message I have to hand back is important for everybody, and if you've got a grandparent— grandfather or grandmother—listen to them. They're the glue to your family. They're the ones who have been through uphill and downhill, problems, situations, issues of any kind that they've had to work through. Listen to them. Don't be sticking them in a home or somewhere and forgetting about them. They got the knowledge. They got the stories. Just because we're all getting gray heads, that's no sign our brain quit working. Some people do get Alzheimer's and different problems, but still, you listen to your elders and the way that they handle situations or anything. It's mostly the elders—every elder has a different story, but an elder has a story.

When my great-aunt Frances, Chief George Harney's sister, lived with us, she talked about funny things. She said, "You got to talk about funny things too, because you have to be funny inside. Tickle the funny bone." That's what she used to say. Not being educated in a white man's world, she knew that laughter had something to do with feeling good, so she had stories and she would laugh. No matter how many times she told them, she would always sit back and laugh and get us all laughing. That was her purpose, to get us all laughing. She would lighten things up. She was always good like that.

I said the Creator was smart, and I teach people that, too. The greatest gift He gave us was life, and the second thing He gave us was this thinkin' thing called the brain. He put it on top of our body to rule the rest of it. How you run that brain is how well you do your life every day. Do you do it begrudgingly? Because if you do, you're gonna get sick. You know, your immune system goes down if you don't put a little sunshine in it. And if you don't have laughter, why not? Laughter is our cheapest medicine, because when you're laughing, your immune system is up, as I say, in the sunshine belt. Your body heals and your brain comes along. If you really care about your life, you will *ha ha ha* sometime during the day, get your spirit up there. That's your job. If you allow yourself to get depressed, you're the one who is runnin' your brain that way. Nobody else can make you do it. That's a powerful tool, our brain. Many people run their brains so strongly that they can will themselves to die, and they do. That's how powerful our brain is.

Sit yourself in a chair across from yourself and look at yourself. What can you do, and what can you change about yourself? Only you can do it. I used to teach that. A person is in a chair, and I say, "Over here in this chair is your other self. Here's a pillow. Do you want to beat him up or her up? Go do it." Use that pillow and thump him up, because you look at yourself, your inner self, and nobody can do it but yourself. Looking inside, are you worthy to be on this planet? Are you worthy to have another breath? Are you worthy to have another day? I am. I've got a lot of work ahead of me yet, and so I feel like the Creator has put me here for that reason. So I'm going around saying, "Wake up. Think about tomorrow. It isn't here yet, but if you run today right, tomorrow will come." We have no way to say if I will wake up tomorrow. I don't know, but I pray so. I pray that I'll wake up tomorrow.

All life can only do one day at a time, all life. I hope that everybody that is reading this, that you have a handle only on one day at a time. I still think that we can make a difference if we keep on, all of us. If you are an elder reading this, use your voice to help your children, to guide them. Live a good life so that when you go to the Star Nation you leave a good legacy for your children to follow. This is what I am doin'. I don't want to ever let my kids think that I was going to go out drinkin' or druggin' or on some kind of a pill. I am going to leave a good legacy to my children so that they'll be proud of who I am and be able to walk in my footsteps as I am walking in my Old Ones' footsteps. I think that if you can kind of watch the way that you do your life in integrity, if you're honest to yourself, you'll be honest to anybody. This is my character. I am honest to myself on everything. Even with my crosswords. I don't peek at the answers and say, "Yeah, I did it all by myself." I don't do that. Even a simple thing like that. I am honest to me, and honesty is one of the great characteristics I have. Another one that I have is kindness. I am kind to everybody; all over the world where I've traveled, I am kind. Little kids come up and hug me, and I don't have to have borne the child to love it; I love them as they come. I have a lot of people call me Grandma, so if you don't have a grandma, you can adopt me. Because if you can adopt a highway, you certainly can adopt a grandma.

There's thirteen of us Grandmothers, and I am the one from Oregon. If you're reading this in Oregon, you can adopt me as your grandma. I try to be a good grandma. I got five generations of children. The five generations are little guys, and I am still teaching their parents, who are young yet, how to take care of their kids. I tell them like I did my children, "I can't give you kindness, laughter, smiles, joy, compassion, and all this inside stuff. That's your inside job. So, if you want any of these kind of things, kindness and love, respect, and all of this, you have to have it so that you can give it away to anybody you meet." This is my philosophy of how to get along in the world. Like the Spirit told me years ago, over and over, "Stop getting mad. It's hard on your heart. You got other things to do." "Yes, Grandfather. Okay, Grandfather." "You don't have to get mad at what you see, what you hear, or what you read." "Thank you, Grandfather. I'll do that." So, I have.

I don't get mad at anybody. I could get mad at something ten times a day, at something I read, something I see. But I don't. I mind as part of my integrity between me and my beloved Creator. I obey those words to the letter, and it's a choice that any of us can make. You don't have to get mad at somebody, cuss them out or something. You got to know your perimeters. You can't change nobody else by you gettin' mad. They might agree with you just to shut you up, but it doesn't stop that anger in them. Or you could thump 'em up and then they say, "Okay, I will," but they don't. You can't change anybody else. Just like, if my son got mad about something, I can't change him. I can say, "Well, you didn't have to do that." As a mother, I could say that. But I don't go getting mad. I could find something to get mad at—what I read, a lot of garbage in the newspapers. The way people are getting treated I could get mad at. But does it change anything? Your anger, does it change anything? I agree with the Creator, it is hard on your heart. Your muscles tense up around your heart when you're angry. It is like your fist wanting to draw up and punch somebody.

I listen to my Creator. Okay, I don't need to get mad about that. I could get mad at my daughter sometimes because she gets pretty strict with me. And I can see why; because she wants me to live. I don't get mad at her because she's had two heart attacks. Could I cause her another one by gettin' angry? I certainly could. So, I don't. I just say, well, she's got a right to ruffle her feathers if she wants. She'll calm down pretty soon. I just pray, "Grandfather, you take care of her, because I can't. You help her, whatever it is." You know, I know where I am limited. There's one God and I am not it. I know that I can't change my adult kids. All I have is the obligation just to pray for them. And prayer works because I believe in my prayer. I don't pray idly. I know where my beloved Creator is. It isn't the doorknob above my head. My Creator is all around me and in me. I have to keep this all clean in my heart so the Beloved can dwell within me. I always say that I have a good sky pilot. How's yours workin'? You want to borrow mine?

People say, "You travel so much by yourself," and I say, "I'm never alone." I am never alone. "Beloved, you come and be with me and keep me safe all the way over there. Keep everything away from my car. Take care of my car tires. Bless you, Mother Earth, for my car." Always I give gratitude to that and to my Creator. I am always thankful. A person gives me a penny, I am thankful. I am not a greedy person. What I need will come.

My daughter don't work. I supply all the money that comes to me and share it with her. Her clothes, her food, the roof over her head, my car. I pay the car; I pay the insurance; I buy the gas, the oil, everything. I will always stretch my money, every day. Every month the Creator helps me to stretch my money. I am so grateful. I don't sit and fuss that tomorrow I got these two bills to pay, am I going to be able to do it and have money left. I don't fuss because I know the Creator will take care of it. That's Beloved's job, to see that the money I need comes and that it will supply all our needs—not our wants, our needs.

I could probably dress pretty fancy, but I do good enough. I am dressing my daughter and me. She is always wanting this and that and I don't sit and fuss with her, "No, you don't need this. No, you could live without that." I go through the denial, "Do I have to have this?" Deny. Denial is not a river in Egypt. Denial is that you can deny yourself, that you don't have to have something like this. What she needs is more important than what I was wanting. That's the way I rationalize stuff. It always works. I am always grateful for how the Creator helps take care of me. Without that, I am nothing. I don't get mad at anything. I don't get mad at what I read, what I see, or what I hear. So I have listened, and I mind. I suppose I could find something to get mad at if I wanted to, but I don't.

So, I hope you think about anger. Everybody has got an anger button, but how you dissipate it is the good thing, how you handle it the best way for yourself. I used to tell my kids, "Watch Muhammad Ali when he boxes in the ring." I said, "He'd get his opponent so mad, he'd tease him and jazz him around and get him so mad that his opponent would lose his footwork; he'd swing, and he'd miss Muhammad Ali." I said, "So, see, anger could interfere with the way that you look and the way that you conduct your physical self." I used to tell my kids, "You watch him. You watch and see how he does it, because every time he got his opponent mad, then Muhammad Ali would always win." So, what's your anger button? And you'll live longer, to boot.

Another thing that I would like to say is that there is a Creator that created all of us, and I am not talkin' church, and I am not talkin' religion. Do you stop at least once a day to give thanks just for being, just for taking up a little spot on Earth Mother's space? Do you give thanks to the Creator for that? Because if you don't, I think you really need to get started doing it. Learn to be grateful. Teach yourself that we are part of the Beloved's creation.

As I grew, I was called to do this spiritual walk. Looking back at all those six or seven chiefs in my background, am I worthy to do this? I argued with my Creator: "I am not worthy. You better give it to somebody else." But it kept coming anyway, so I accepted the guidance of the Creator on my spiritual walk. I pray today that I have said something that will make you think about yourself and how you do in your life. Are you doin' it right? Check it out; check yourself out and see. Can you do a better job? I pray so, and I pray that I have encouraged you to think about some of these things. I pray that I have made you an instant teacher, that you can teach this to your family, to your children, to your grandchildren, to your neighbors, to the school system.

I had people in Australia say, "Gee, we're grey-headed, Grandma. What could we do?" I said, "I don't care if you're grey-headed. Your brain still works. Teach the kids in the school some of the things that you have experienced. You can still be useful and teach kids." So, they have. They have gone into the school systems over there. And I will go back over there again this year to keep them encouraged.

It was the same way in New Zealand and all the other places around the world; clear down in Mapiá, in the rainforests in South America, in Rio de Janeiro, and over in Europe—you name it. You know, I am saying these same things to the many, many people around the globe. More voices of truth, past and present, are all needed. The more voices, the better support for the habitat that we all live in. Air, land, and water—everything. The animals, all of it. We all need to care about it and take care of it. It is up to us as two-leggeds, as I like to call us, to think about what we're doin' and how we can do better. Maybe you could change your path, get on this good Red Road and make a good trail and a good path for all of those that are coming behind you, like the Old Ones did for me; it took them all to make who I am. I pray that I, too, am doin' what they want me to do so that I can carry on, and carry on the good things they left me with. I still hear their voices in the wind instructing me on things, reminding me, "Do this. Don't do that." I still listen because the Creator gave me two ears and one mouth so that I could hear all that and speak about it. So, thank you ever so much for listening. Have a good day.

5

MY SPIRITUAL WALK – A VOICE FOR THE VOICELESS

As I said before, my native name is Taowhywee. It came to me when I was young, and I didn't want to accept it because I wasn't worthy. I felt to take such a beautiful, gracious name of my great-grandmother—she was a very strong medicine woman in Southern Oregon. Her name was Taowhywee, which means "Morning Star." The name kept coming and kept coming, and I said, "Oh, okay. But you got to help me from the other side. You help me, Grandmother, and guide me and nudge me when I need it, because I am going to go on a spiritual path for my beloved Creator." Looking back at all those six or seven chiefs in my background, am I worthy to do this? I argued with my Creator, "I am not worthy. You better give it to somebody else." But anyway, it kept coming, so I accepted the guidance of the Creator on my spiritual walk. Even then I thought, am I doing it right so that they will be proud of me as I walk in their footsteps? So, when I took the name Taowhywee, I thought, "Oh, my. Will they be proud of me for doing that?" You know, that was a good thing in my life.

Here I am, ninety years old and soon to be ninety-one. Here I am today, the oldest living descendant of those beautiful, wonderful people that are all gone on now. Yet I honor them because it took all of them to make who I am. So, you up there, I pray,

"Thank you for who I am. Thank you for being in my life and in my heart and in my mind. Bless you all, and you are waiting for me, I know. But not yet. I have lots to do." I have been busy with our world, our environment all over the world, to the point where my tribe deemed me a living legend to the tribe. I feel very honored to have that indelible marking on my back. Wherever I travel, there's my Confederated Tribe, the Siletz. I really thank my beloved Creator for all the things that I have done, and I pray that there is a smile on each continent, that I am doing the right things. I give thanks that He put me on this path a long time ago.

One day Spirit told me I had to be a voice for the voiceless. Oh, dear god. I couldn't get it straight in my mind what that meant. I kept pondering it. Then it would come to me again and again and again. I got kind of frustrated with what the Beloved wanted me to do, to be a voice for the voiceless. I was still kind of young yet. One day I was sitting out on my deck in front of my house, and I had a stand there with a glass of water on it. My big dog was laying down by my feet. His name was Segat, which in the Yurok tribe means "coyote." He was part pit bull, so he would watch out for me, just follow me everywhere. Anyway, I was sitting there and thinking about being a voice for the voiceless. I was shaking my head. I didn't know what that meant. The wind started blowing, and I heard the leaves in the tree rustling, and I thought, "Oh, the wind, the air—it doesn't have a voice. Oh, Grandfather, is that what you mean? The air. We cannot live without it." Just then, I stopped and reached over and got my glass of water, and my eyes went right to that water in that glass, and I thought, "Huh, you don't have a voice either. The water doesn't have a voice. Oh, I am understanding, Grandfather. I can understand now." Just then, my big dog stood up and laid his head on my knee, and I went, "You don't have a voice, either. The animal kingdom. Oh, Grandfather, yes. Now I know. Thank you for being patient with me." Took me so long to understand. I guess I am thick-headed, but anyway, now I know.

So I began my life traveling. People hired me all over the world to be a voice for the voiceless, teaching people that we have to be a voice for all these things, to watch out for our air, to watch out for our water and stop the pollution, to watch out for the animal kingdom. And Grandfather said, "I have given you all the earth, everything you need for your survival. You are to take care of it and use it in moderation and in balance." "Oh, Grandfather, we've walked away from those teachings." There's a hole in our ozone layer now. There's pollution in our rivers and streams and oceans. There is pollution and smog in our cities, and in many cities we can't see the sky. I have been to some of those cities. I've been to Los Angeles. When we get down there, my eyes are running with tears because of the pollution. I have been to India, where you couldn't see the sky, and Mexico City, and many other places. We are putting so much cement on the green of Mother Earth's face that we're damaging our own selves. I began traveling all over the world, teaching people to join me and be a voice for the voiceless, teaching that the animals need us to care for their habitat. So many things are happening that we need to take care of.

6
INTERNATIONAL GRANDMOTHERS

As I said, my Native name, Taowhywee, was given to me a long time ago through my great-grandmother Margaret, whose name was Morning Star. She was a great shaman of the Takelma people here in Southern Oregon. I am very honored to be here today to say these words; in order to carry on, my words are my work. We have to encourage the young people to get involved if we're going to make a difference. Whether it be in taking care of Earth Mother or whether it is a carrying on of words of wisdom, we need to enlighten our young people so that they, too, can carry these messages to their homes and to their families and to those generations yet to come. I feel very good today to be able to state some of the things about my life. I pray that it is all of us at any age, young and old, to carry the message that I am leaving behind here today.

Us Grandmas were called. Some people said they heard of me and watched my walk in Southern Oregon for four and a half years, so they called me and wanted to know if I wanted to come to New York and be with these Grandmas. It took a few weeks for me to pray, and finally I accepted. We came together on October 11, 2004, out of Phoenicia, New York, first time in the history of the world. After we sat down for a while, my Grandma Mona Polacca from Arizona said, "We've all come here. We are going to formalize this group." Through it all, she said, "It is the eleventh hour; we need to be coming together." So they did, and then they nominated me, as the oldest of the group, as the chair.

We left there, and then we went inland to a beautiful place called Menlo Park, where the Dalai Lama—the monks and the lamas—all come for their retreat. It was a great gathering for us Grandmas that came from all over the world. My Grandmas are Bernadette Rebienot from Gabon, Africa; Julieta Casimiro from Huautla de Jimenez, Mexico; and Maria Alice Campos Freire and Clara Shinobu Iura from the Amazon Rainforest in Brazil. Then over in Katmandu, Nepal, we have Aama Bombo, and Tsering Dolma Gyaltong is from Tibet. We have Mona Polacca from Phoenix, Arizona. "Polacca" means butterfly. And there is my Mayan Grandma, Flordemayo, who now is living in Estancia, New Mexico. Then I have two Grandmas out in the Black Hills of South Dakota, Beatrice Long Visitor Holy Dance and Rita Long Visitor Holy Dance. Then I have Margaret Behan in Lame Deer, Montana, and Rita Pitka Blumenstein of the Yup'ik tribe in Alaska, and I am from Oregon. All very special women in their own right.

Each one of these beautiful ladies walks with a different medicine, and we all get along. For example, I was in South America with Grandma Maria Alice. They have this Santo Daime religion down there, and I was standing in line with all these people to partake of the waters that come from the bark of this tree that they cook. I speak to my beloved Creator and say, "Grandfather, this tree that they use for their medicines is from our Earth Mother, but I don't have it in my land. I haven't been raised with this tree that they get the medicine from, but that's my sister Grandma, so I am going to take some of this medicine, too. So I would like for you to bless me, too, because I am going to join my sister Grandma and her people here. So, bless me, too, with it, Grandfather. Thank you." That's what I do with all the other Grandmas with their medicines. Us Grandmas who came together in 2004, it was the first time in the history of the world that these women gathered, and I said at that time, "We are going to raise a femininity to the top wherever we go." Because it was, in the beginning, a goddess world; then it went patriarchal.

Now it is slowly turning back to a goddess world. More and more women are stepping up, taking prestigious jobs. Even here in Oregon we have a woman governor. I am happy to be able to say that. I think that more and more women are going to be steppin' up, taking these prestigious jobs, because we are natural nurturers. I say we have this invisible umbilical cord to the earth. We care. We are the givers of life, and we've always been the givers of life. I think the world is going to slowly turn back to a goddess world. This is why I think we have wars: because inside of every male is his woman consciousness, his female part—it needs to balance. I believe it's not balanced inside, and this is why we have wars from these guys. I think that's what us Grandmas have to do. Take the women, the Pakistani women, that have to cover up. The men can lie and say the women didn't have their veils on or something, and then the women get killed. It is not right. Because a woman didn't say that, a man said that. This empowerment has got to stop the women being put down. Those men over there, swamis and all, they have got to start to change and give more respect to a woman's body. They have just as much right to stand up in the world as a man does; more so, because they gave the man the right to come into the world.

Men, you've got this feminine part inside of you, and it is not a sign of weakness. It's a sign of balance in you when you admit that it took a woman's body to bring you into this world in the first place. So, you have to be grateful to Mom for giving you life. And if you're not grateful to Mom, why not? What's wrong with you that you can't say, "Thanks, Mom, for my life," because there's no way that you can obliterate that beginning world of yours; it took her body to get you here. There's a fifty-cent word that you have to do, and that is *acceptance*. Accept that "yes, it took a woman's body to bring me into the world." I think when you do that, you give yourself a different perspective, a different outlook on who you are through that admission.

Whether you love your mom or not is irrelevant. Truth is, she gave you life, however you cut it. When you admit it, even if you can't tell her, "Thanks for my life," you can say it in your own way to yourself. And if you've got a daughter, she came from a woman's body. Same with Grandma—came from a woman's body—and Grandpa. All of those that are behind you, it took a woman's body to bring them into the world. This is why I say us Grandmas have this invisible umbilical cord to the earth, because we care. We have all known that. We accept that because women, like I said, are natural nurturers. We care about our environment because we have given life to children, and of course every mother wants her child to live. I am a great-great-great-great-grandma, and I want all of my little children to grow up and get grey-headed like me and have good air, good water.

So I am not greater than or lesser than; I am doin' what I am supposed to be doin' here on this planet, helping people to get along, helping people to find peace, helping people to find laughter and joy, helping people to accept just for being, just for having life. It's called gratitude. Many people can't even say they're grateful for their life, and it is sad. It is sad that they can't say, "Thanks for my life. Thanks, because I just take up this itty bitty spot on the Earth Mother's face. Thank you for all that you have given me all these years, all the food, the clothing, everything for my existence. Bless you." You know, it's gratitude just for being.

If people could understand that, it'd be so much easier to stick with things, and how they run that thing, and how they'd be in their body, how they'd get along with their family, how they'd love their kids or not love their kids. How you run this thinkin' thing is who you are. That's why I say the hardest journey ever made is the fourteen inches from this thinkin' thing to your heart. Once you can get there, you have thought of all of this. You have rationalized it. You have accepted it when you get here. Like I say, the *ah ha* stage. "*Ah ha*, now I know who I am." I don't care who you are or what color your skin is, because if you can do that, then you're 100 percent in my book, because it tells me you're grateful to take another breath. You're grateful to wake up in the morning and say, "*Ah ha*! One more day."

I teach kids, everybody, that everything that has life can only do one day at a time. This is why I say it is no coincidence, us Grandmas coming together like that. You know, in the beginning it was a goddess world, then it went patriarchal. Now it is slowly turning; more and more women are standing up. Oregon's got a woman governor, Kate Brown, first time in history. She's got a brain, and she uses it well. Not just for women, but for the men, too, and laws and freedom and peace. She's got it. If she didn't, she wouldn't be there. I just say to Beloved, "You're sure helping me and the state, backing me up and taking prestigious jobs."

Inside of every female is a male consciousness that needs to balance in us so that we won't become so bossy and jumping and hollering around. Knowing what I know about how the Creator jumps in and helps me, you know . . . looking back, I could see where He has had His hand on me way back there, telling me, "Do this, do this, do this." It is like trying to tell me to play hopscotch—you do it this way.

It needs to balance. I believe that us women coming together, us Grandmothers, are empowering women and elders. And for you young people that put your elders out to pasture, remember, they're the glue to your family. They are the glue to your community. We care. Grandmothers care. Just because we don't work 24/7, that's no sign you can push us aside. We each got a different story, a survival story. We each care about all of our children and about giving life. I believe us thirteen Grandmas got an invisible umbilical cord to the Mother Earth, that we are natural nurturers. We care about our water, our earth, everything. Just because I don't have a Bengal tiger here, or the rhino, or the elephant, or the apes, is no sign that I cannot pray for them right here, ask the Creator to take care of the habitat of these beautiful creatures that He put here on this planet for us to watch over.

You could do the same. Think about it. Add the animal kingdom into your prayer, and care about our Earth Mother that has sustained us. The clothes you've got on your back today—listen to me—it came from the Mother Earth. If you've got jewelry, that comes from the beauty out of her, also. How about your car? All of it came from her, too. The plane you ride in is all from Mother Earth. Have you learned to give thanks for all of this? If not, you should. Your house was built from the one-legged, all of the frame. And do you think of the Tree People, the one-leggeds, for your home? Even though the tree is dead, do you give thanks? Because the spirit is still there. I don't know whether anybody told you, but they say if you need energy, hug a tree. If your house is built from a wood frame, thank it, bless it. The head of your bed, the chair you sit in, the table you eat at, all of these things come from the one-legged—the Tree People, I call them. And just because I don't live by the redwood trees anymore is no sign that I leave them out of my prayer. I pray that the Cloud People will come and water them so that the water can get clear to the top of the tree. If it doesn't, then the top dies, and then the beetles get in it and it kills the tree. So just because a redwood tree isn't in your backyard, don't stop praying for them because they are all part of the environment, also.

I get calls to pray for the pygmy elephants. Some time ago, a young man called me and said, "Grandma, pray for me. There are so few of the pygmy elephants. I want to bring them back." I said, "You can. You just pray and it'll work out for you." So now he has got over a hundred pygmy elephants, and so it works. It's my obligation as a minister and as a person that somebody don't have to be right here in front of me for me to pray for them. I can send long-distance prayers over there because I know they work. My youngest son and his wife lived out of Taft, what they call Lincoln City, in Oregon. I was down in Grants Pass, and they called me up and said, "Mom, you got to get up here." "Why have I got to get up there? I can't do it. I am busy. What's wrong?" "Somebody keeps trying to break into my house, and if you come up here and smudge it and pray for it, it'll stop." I said, "Well, I can't do it right now. But," I said, "I will go out and do some prayers right

now. When we get done talkin', I will go and do that right now."
So I did. I went out on the porch, and I lit my smudging bowl
up. I stood out there on the deck, and I blew the smoke, and I
prayed and told the Creator, "You take it that way around his
house, and You circle it inside and out, and take care of it for me,
because I can't go right now, as You know." I did all that. So about
an hour later he calls me up. "What did you do?" I said, "What
do you mean, what did I do?" He said, "When we got down to
the house, we could smell the smudge all around the house, and
we got inside and there was more of it. What did you do?" I said,
"Don't thank your mother. I am just asking the Creator to go up
there and take care of your house. So it's done. Okay?" My son is
gone, but his wife remembers this. She was with him.

My oldest boy, Robert, was living in Jacksonville, Wyoming.
His wife called up and said he was dying. Something happened
to him when he worked at Knott's Berry Farm in California. He
was the top welder. He welded those big *zip zip* things, you know?
And those boats that go in the water and they spin—he put the
pipes up for the air to shoot up under the boats so they turn
like that. He did all that, and one day he fell off of a scaffold. It
nearly killed him. It hurt his back, and the doctors had him on
morphine for a long time, which goofed up his liver. That is what
finally got him, was his pain pills. His wife said, "He can't even
talk to you on the phone because he is just whispering." I said,
"Sharon, go get his prayer feathers." I had sent him some white
tail-of-the-eagle feathers, you know, for prayer feathers. "Go get
his prayer feathers and put them in his hand. Then you put that
phone up to his ear 'cause I'm gonna pray. He doesn't have to try
to talk. I will just do my prayers. You hold it up there. When you
are ready, let me know." Pretty soon she called me back. "He's got
them in his hand, and I got the phone put to his ear." So I prayed
with my boy and told him that the Creator said, "Not now." I
said, "He's not going to take you yet. He's going to help you. So
you believe these words." I was praying, you know. Then she put
the phone up and put the feathers away. She said that he didn't

even have the strength to put any volume into his voice so I could hear it. I said "He's going to rise, Sharon. Be patient."

About three days go by, and I am over in Crescent City. I have to go to Smith River because my son Keith was coming from McKinleyville and I was going to meet him up there. They're going to help those Tolowa people; they're going to do a dance. Three days after I had done that prayer for my oldest boy, here's this big ol' voice on my phone, "Hello, Mother." I said, "Keith, what are you doing? I thought you were supposed to go help Lauren up the Smith River at church?" "Mother, who do you think this is?" I said, "Keith?" "No, Mother. This is Robert." So the tears run down my face, tears of gratitude for my beloved Creator that took care of my son. He didn't die then. It was a long time after that.

We Grandmothers have a purpose, and we each have a different story, but we got a story. We each are empowered with strength, and we've been doing good things where we come from. I don't believe this is some idle thing. I think the Creator is in the mix of this, that it is meant to be. I believe that women are going to start taking prestigious jobs all over the world and empowering themselves, and grandmothers are going to be stepping up because of us. Now, I don't get the big head, but it is true, that is the way I feel. We have this purpose to empower women all over the globe. This is why we are all from different places all over the world. Of the thousands and thousands of people in Oregon, why me? Creator must have had a hand in this.

When we Grandmas were all together, the interpreter was telling my Grandma, "Look at you guys. Thousands of people out of Jojutla, Mexico," and Grandma Julieta was chosen out of all of those millions of people down there because she's been doing a great job praying and helping her people. The same way with Aama Bombo, when she was making medicine for hundreds of people every day, helping people to get strong and teaching them how to take care of themselves. She has been doing this ever since she was a young girl. The Creator had His hand on her or she wouldn't be doing all this all these years. Our Grandma Rita Pitka Blumenstein, from Alaska, she's a doctor. Right now they have all of her plants growing out there between these hospitals, and they're using them. They're all labeled, big stands to tell what they are, what they are used for.

Each one of these Grandmas had been special in their world. The Tibetan Grandma, Tsering Dolma Gyaltong, and her teachings since she was a little girl . . . you could feel how they were all raised up in age and how the Creator had His hand on them to bring them to this point where we gathered. You could feel that. I said, "What a beautiful flower we made for the Creator, all of us. All the colors around the globe." People said yellow was over here, the black was down there, the redskins over here, the whites over there. Ah ha! I think the Creator had us all deformed because even in the white man's Bible it says, "Go cleave onto another and make me a new flower garden." And we've done that. "Ladies," I am telling the Grandmas, "we have done that. We are all different colors. We are a beautiful flower to our beloved Creator, right here. And we're doin' His work whether we knew it or not. Trying to make people better where we live, to feel better, to think of themselves better." I said, "Everything that you've been doin' is what the Creator is wanting us to do to help people to grow and to care about themselves, to be happy with who they are, to accept life and to care about themselves so that they have a purpose in their community, to be a voice."

The greatest voice that we adults can have is to make a better path for the little ones coming after us. It is our obligation as adults, no matter what age, to preserve, to take care so that the little people can grow up and be healthy and have the same opportunities as we have. Think about it. What can you do? If us Grandmothers, as old as all of us are, can do all these things, what is your excuse? You need to get in there and help us and be a voice—a voice for the voiceless—and help take care of your habitat where you live. Do as best you can. This is why I work like I do all over the world. And all of us Grandmas care. We're all concerned about water. And another thing: I say every one of us are your voice because wherever we've come from, us Grams—I as the oldest and I think our Grandma Mona Polacca is the youngest—we care about all the things. We care about the fracking. We care about taking the tops off of mountains. We care about the plants that give us good medicine.

From the get-go, people from pharmacies came to our Native people a long, long time ago, hundreds of years ago, and stayed with the tribal people searching out the medicine plants. They took the plants and they made the medicine, but they never gave any of us a dime for that. The medicines are there. We pray that you, that anybody that we talk to, is using good medicine. If you have to have medicine, it's the good stuff. Abusing it is another thing. Don't abuse your medicine. Only use it through the doctor's instructions.

I always say I am your voice. As I journey the globe, I care about all these things because I care about our oceans; I care about our rivers and streams; I care about the ice in Iceland and Greenland that is melting so rapidly. Maybe I won't see the water rising, but it is going to happen because of the emissions that we have here. I say that we must have scientists that could put water in your gas tank, drop in a pill, and drive that car from the West Coast to the East Coast. Stop the emissions. Airplanes are letting stuff out through emissions. Is it good for us to be breathing that stuff that they're doing? Why are we doin' all of these things? The spraying—why are we spraying this tetraphosphate and 2,4-D all around? It is going to get in somebody's well. It is going to get in the creeks. I used to go fishing in Lake Selmac, and it was a half a mile away that they were spraying. I told Wildlife Fish and Game, "When I go fishing, I would like to be able to eat my catch. And if that stuff gets into Lake Selmac, I won't be able to go fishing and eat my catch." It's that way everywhere—they're spraying this stuff along the highways, along your house. Wherever you use this stuff, it's god-awful. Switzerland manufactured that tetrazine, and they banned it years ago. None of the European countries are using that stuff over there, but India bought up the formula and they're selling it. So we got ahold of some of it over here, and they were using it along the highways and spraying up in the mountains. It is certainly going to ruin somebody's water.

It's frightening to me what we're doing. Realize what is biodegradable. Do we need biodegradable? Of course we do. Whether it is detergents or whether it is something that we are rubbing on our baby. You know, what's in that stuff? Is it good for baby? Being able to read your label is an important thing, I think, for your own health and for anybody's health. We need to be more cognizant of what's going on around us. Be a voice. I think the Creator gave us a whisper and put a little volume to it so that we could be a voice, a voice for the voiceless. Like being a voice for the animal kingdom; we can't live on this planet without the animal kingdom. It's a balance. We need the balance. Think about it.

And stop the garbage in the rivers and streams. We got all the dams off the Rogue River now, so watch what you're putting in the river. There's life in that water. Let's take care of them and be that voice for the trout, the fish in the waters, the crawfish, whatever is out there. Even the oceans, you know, the whales and orcas, the octopus, all of that life that's out there; the ocean is part of our balance. We need to be a voice. We need to take care of their habitat, all habitat. We need to stand up and take care of it.

This is our job. This is where we're obligated—how to take care of the habitat of all these things. I thought about the habitat, with garbage and stuff being dumped around here in Josephine County that is laced with industrial waste, and human feces being dumped, creating all kinds of slimy growth in the rivers. I have thought about that, too, that they should not be doing that. We need to put our garbage in a place where it is safe for all life. This is the thing that we need to be doin'. Think about those things. Think about pollution. It is us that are polluting the ocean. It is us that are polluting the rivers and streams. We need to stop, because there is life in that water, and we have the voice to do it. So, let's police the waters, let's police the oceans and the rivers.

If you live on the bank of the river anywhere in Oregon, watch. Don't let people be dumpin' stuff in it, because we have to be that voice for the swimmers in the water, take care of them, and take care of all habitat for all things. The Creator came to me a long time ago and said that He's given us all, everything we need for our existence, but to take care of it and use it in balance and moderation. We've walked away from those teachings. We need to walk back and start being a voice for all these things, and stop what is wrong, stop what we're doing. Stop the pollution so that our little kids and your grandkids' grandkids and the unborn— the next seven generations—have a good life here in this land.

We always said if we're going to make a difference, we have to start with the young so that when we are gone the youth ambassadors can carry on. My great-granddaughter Shantelle Rilatos, she wanted to be a youth ambassador, and she was a good one. We have many of them. We have one from South Dakota; we have one from South America, one from Alaska—several young women, young girls, they come with us to be youth ambassadors. That means they excel in school, they excel in their life, they are walking a good path, and they can carry on a good message of what it means to be a youth ambassador.

My great-grandson Tyee Rilatos calls me "GG." That stands for "great-grandma," the two Gs. He came to me several years back, and he said, "GG, why is it only girls are ambassadors? Why can't boys be ambassadors?" And I said, "You know what, Great-Grandson, you are doing a good walk. You are doing good in school and you do good in your life." He was just a little guy, and I said, "You have to ask all the rest of the Grandmas about being a youth ambassador. I accept you, but I am only one of us. You need to talk to them."

At that time, for a few weeks I got a Lincoln Navigator I rented out of Grants Pass, and I went over towards Murphy and got a trailer, hitched 'em up. I got his mother to put in the luggage, and we all loaded up and headed for Lame Deer, Montana. And off we went. We got there in three days. I told him, "Bring your drum," because Tyee was already singing with his drum. I have given him lots of drums, and so have other people. When we were finally all together there in this great big room he asked them, "Could I be a youth ambassador?" He stood and he told them why he wanted to be a youth ambassador. I could've kicked myself that I didn't have a recorder to record it, because his mother never gave him words to say. His grandma, my daughter, and myself, who were with him, he didn't talk to us about anything of what he should ask or what he should say. But you know, he stood up, and if there was a Creator that I could see, I knew the Creator was there with him. I could feel that. And the words just rolled out of him why he wanted to be a youth ambassador.

We were all crying, and then Tyee picked up his drum, and he sang them a beautiful song. The Grandmas all gave him a standing ovation and accepted him. It was a great thing how he behaved around over there. We never told him to go and work or doing anything there. We would catch him working, cleaning tables, setting up chairs, rolling silverware, getting the linen and piling it up. That night we went lookin' for him. There he was; he was sleeping on top of all of the sheets and stuff piled out there for them to take and wash. He was tired. But anyway, he had fun. He got Grandma from Katmandu, Aama Bombo, up to the pool table, showed her how to shoot pool. God, we were laughin' till we cried. It was so funny how she laughed. Laugh and laugh and laugh. Talk about good medicine watching them! It was funny because everybody was laughing for his Grandma Aama Bombo to be shooting pool with him.

Tyee's not a little guy. He's over six foot and he is over two hundred pounds. He's a big guy, and now he is going on eighteen years old. He's up to my tribe in Siletz, Oregon, learning our language, getting good grades. All the people who sit on my committee speak about him and how good he is with what he's doing with his life, that he is doing good in school. A long time ago, when he was little, I talked to him about having kindness and compassion and love inside himself, so he does that. He gets kindness back, and I tell him about all those good things. He has a good sense of humor, too.

Tyee's a good peer. He helps the other kids. We talked to him a long time ago about the behavior of bullies and that we never wanted to hear about him being a bully even though he is a big kid. He never was a bully. He was talking to others; he's always good to help others, his classmates. He is a good young man ambassador to us Grandmas. He's doing good with his world like a young man should be. I can see him someday maybe bein' a medicine man. That would be good because he's making good medicine for him and his youth and his era of young people that surround him. I am very proud of him.

He's truthful, too. He is not a liar. He doesn't take anything that doesn't belong to him, which is called stealing. I help him with clothes, shoes, and things all the time, whenever I can, and I do things for him. It is really good, those kids. His sister, who is already an ambassador, has been a teacher for two years, and she is young yet. She has been teaching over in Crescent City, California, at the Yurok language, and so I am really proud of our kids and all of our ambassadors that are doing good in their world. They walk their talk, meaning they are doing good in their world and they're working.

Our Grandma Maria Alice has a hospital down there in the Amazon where she sends her medicines from her plants that they gather, and they make medicine from the plants. She ships it all over the world. What is beautiful about that is that the government helps support her on that and allows her to do that for her income. I've been down there. She brings in a lot of young people to learn hands-on about the plants and the raising of the plants, what they're for, how to make medicine from them, how to pound some of them and put them into poultices—you name it. She is doing good with her big clinic that she has down there. I have been down there with her, right on the Amazon, telling the boatman to clean up the river.

I carried on to people down there about the same things that I've been talking here about, too. Even though they speak Portuguese, they have interpreters that speak their language so they can interpret what I say and give it to them. The things that I talk about here is what I've talked about down there and all over the world. I believe that the young people will be the ones to carry on after us Grandmas.

When we came together in 2004, each one of us Grandmas walked with a different medicine, all from our Mother Earth. So, like I did with my sister Grandma in the Amazon when I drank her juice from the tree, I did that with Grandma Margaret Behan in Montana, who has peyote. I went up and did the same kind of prayer. It's a plant from our Earth Mother. I have not grown up with it. I don't know about it. I have never used it. But there again is my sister Grandma, so, "Bless me, too, Grandfather, when I get up and drink some of it." I did that because each of them walk with a different medicine, but the medicines they walk with is all from our Earth Mother. Down on her land in Estancia, Mexico, Grandma Flordemayo has these great big greenhouses with all medicine plants in them. It's the men that take care of that when it's harvest time. She has plants and stuff from Africa that the African people no longer can use, but she has got some of those plants down there that they manufacture and use. The plants that she has down there in her great big greenhouses, some of it is for your heart, some for cancer, some for all different other things.

I admire them for all they're doin'. I've been down there. I've blessed those places and the medicine that she's growing and that they sell all over the country. So, I admire our Grandmas. Even our Grandma from Alaska, Rita Blumenstein, in between the hospitals—the two big buildings—is a garden, and in that garden are all these plants that Grandma Rita has grown up with and taught about since she was a little girl. She is going on eighty now, and when she was little they gathered these plants. She knew since she was young, 'cause her grandma taught her and her mother how and what the plants were, how to prepare them, and what their uses were. Now here she is a great-gram, and she has got this garden in between the hospitals. They have a little stand above each plant, and it explains what the plant is and what it is used for. The doctors use them.

She has always gathered her plants. Well now, a year or two ago she fell. I said, "You promise me that you'll never go looking for your plant medicines by yourself. You take somebody with you. You take your granddaughter with you so you won't be out there alone, because if you fall and get hurt and you're out there alone, my god, you could die. So, you don't go out there and gather your medicines anymore by yourself." So she promised me.

Now all the other Grandmas, they have different medicines all over the globe. People ask me what is mine. I say, "All of it. Everything, down to a little blade of grass. It's all sacred to me. All of it. It is all needed for us, everybody on this planet. No matter where my feet put me down, that is my place to thank the Creator for all the medicine that comes from that state or that country. I thank the Creator for letting us have these plants wherever we go, you know, so it is great. It is good.

It's up to all of us at any age, young and old, to be able to carry the message that I've been leaving behind here today for all of us. Like His Holiness the Dalai Lama. He has worked hard since he was a young little guy. I was over in India with our Grandma Tsering Gyaltong, who sits in our circle. This beautiful lady had us come to India to be with His Holiness up on the mountain over there. And it was such a treat, a blessed thing that we got to be with him and his people. You know, I can see why he travels and works and gets funds for his talks and things all over the world, because he has over two thousand orphans, and they have a nunnery for the young girls.

They have the houses for all of these little young boys, too. And they have men and women parents in each of these houses to watch after these orphans, and they all have to be fed, they all have to be clothed. They all have to be taught so that they can grow up and be useful and learn a trade, go to school, and the teachers have to be paid to teach all of these orphans. It takes a lot of money, and I see why he travels so much for them. He was driven out of Tibet a long time ago, and our Grandma Tsering Gyaltong was one of the women that did the diversion and helped get His Holiness out of Tibet. They got the highest mountains in the world, and they came through in the dark. It was meant to be for him to get out, because he came across the roughest ground in the mountain, covered in snow. In the dark they traveled to get him out, and I think it was a great thing. It was meant to be for him to get out of Tibet and do the things that he's done. It is like what's happened to us First Nation people in this land, how that came about. We were just about destroyed, like his people, where you had to stop doing your culture and stop your language. You had to stop all the things that was part of your culture to be able to stay in Tibet. But he got out, and I am glad because then he had a place for the orphans that came. They helped teach them their language and teach them their way of life as Tibetan people, to carry on, to be who they are, to be Tibetan people. They had to hire people to come in and teach them all a trade. To have teachers to teach them the language and their traditions takes a lot of money. And it is like us, you know, how we were stripped of all of this, and we weren't allowed to speak our language. We had to leave all of the cultural stuff behind. They wouldn't let us dance in our regalia or speak our language. We were stripped of all of that, and it is similar to what happened to the Tibetan people that got out of Tibet.

I think it was a great honor to be able to go and meet His Holiness the Dalai Lama and to hear his story. When I was going over there I thought, what do you take as a gift to a man like that? I had just beaded a condor feather the night before, and the next day, when I was packing, my eye kept going to the condor feather, and I thought, do I take that over there to him? I ended up taking the condor feather with me, and I thought, don't you get me in trouble now. I am going to put you in my suitcase. It's like a brother to me, the condor feathers that I carry. So, I took this one to give to His Holiness.

When I was up there on the mountain, it kind of shocked me when he came out of the temple to join all thirteen of us Grandmas. There was all of these soldiers with camouflage suits and their rifles all around him. I felt sad for him that he only could travel that way to be safe. What a gracious person that man is, full of compassion and love for everybody of all ages, how he travels making good medicine all over the world for his people and does the things he does. Because he has to keep everybody fed and clothed, and medicines, doctors, teachers, books to study—all of this is on his shoulders, to be able to gather the funds to let those little kids be raised up right. I was there, and if you want to see some of them, then get our DVD of us Grandmas. It is in our film, and it shows all of the orphans, how they're dressed. Many of them ran up to us Grandmas and begged us to take them home. I cried. I cried because so many of them wanted to come with us. My heart goes out to His Holiness. When I handed him that condor feather, he put his head down and he was blessing it. You could hear him. I couldn't understand the words, but he was talking to the feather with his head down. My head was down, too, and that picture went all over the country of him and I with a condor feather.

I always admire the strength and the courage that it takes for His Holiness to travel the world and to keep the funds flowing in. So, if you're reading this, he needs you to help him, because he has a lot of mouths to feed and to clothe and to educate. He teaches them jobs, and many of them come back after they get educated; they come back with their skills and their knowledge to teach other young ones coming through.

When we were there, some of them crossing the border got killed, and every store and everything in that town shut down, and it's a sad thing to see. We were there. They get a lot of snow over there, and they have a lot of storms that come, and they have to plow the snow away so that they can get out in the winter to go visit their neighbor. They have a really hard time and a hard life. But it's a beautiful thing that India has moved over and let the Tibetan people have a place where they can come and flourish, to learn, and to care for one another. I just admire the government of India for them being able to do that. And His Holiness works hard, so send your prayers out for him, too, and his people. Maybe pray to China's government so that they can soften down, so that the Tibetan people can get home.

I don't think it's right, what China has done to the Tibetan Nation. They're the only ones who know how to live up in those mountains, to exist at that altitude. So, now they've been stripped of everything, and China is taking over everything, won't let those that had to stay and couldn't get out—China made them stop their culture and traditions; they had to learn to speak Chinese and do the Chinese way, and I don't think it's right. So join me in prayers to the Chinese government, that they could think about it and soften down and let the Tibetan people go home. I pray that I have impressed something upon your life, upon you, that you can do. Join me in prayers to help His Holiness the Dalai Lama.

Us Grandmas came together where they go to have the retreat over there in New York; it was a beautiful place where they had us come. Us Grandmas came for the first time in the history of the world, lifting our voices up for all the things and the habitats, to take care of the habitats of all living things so that we can all live here in the seven generations yet to come. So, use your voice and speak out against some of the things that are happening. Watch what is happening in the habitats of all things. Stop the silence. The wolves, the coyotes, and all the animals have a right to make their sounds. The orcas and all the whales that we have, they have a right to make their sounds. So stop the silence. I have a pin that I wear a lot of times, "Stop the Silence," to let them come home.

7
WATER

Guard your water. Love your water, because it's in your body. It can hear you when you talk to it, and you need to thank it for your life every day. Every day you get up, bless the water for your life. Years ago I was called by Dr. Barbara Smit to Switzerland. "Grandma, we'd sure like you to come over here to bless the Rhine River because it's so polluted. Could you do that?" I sent word back, "Yes, I will come, Dr. Barbara." So we met up on this beautiful hillside, and down below was the Rhine River. I told her before I came to have about four bowls. They don't have to be glass, just something to hold water, and I'll have some of the menfolk or young folk go down and get some water, over half full in each one.

I got there and got to meet everybody, and they knew who I was and why I came. There was hundreds and hundreds and hundreds of people. I had those young people go down and get those bowls filled with water. They said they could get a bucket and pour it. I said, "Uh huh. I want each bowl separately to be dipped in the water, and you bring it back up." So they did, and we had four big, long tables to set the bowls of water on.

The people lined up, and I stood there at the microphone and told them about being water babies. "You're all water babies. You are all born in the amnio sac in water, and water is our first medicine. Water can hear. I don't know if anybody has ever told any of you that, but water can hear. Seventy-five percent of your body is water. Do you say hello to it and thank it for your life? I bet you don't." I said, "There is water in your spit. There's water in your blood. There's water in your tears. Then you got all these thousands of little brain cells; each one needs to be coated with water." I said, "They kind of act like points in a car. You have to have good water to connect. Think of that. When you come up here to the water and you've never talked to the water before, this is a great opportunity for you to learn. All you got to do is just say, 'Forgive me, but from now on I'll thank you whenever I use you, whether it's washing my hands, taking a shower, washing my car, washing my clothes, cooking, flushing the toilet.' Wherever you use water, thank it for you having it. Think of how we would all smell right now if we didn't have water to bathe." I said to them, "Just think how our clothes would look if we didn't have water to wash them and make them clean. Think about it. Think about how much water—is it four hundred gallons a day or more that you use in your household? Think about it. How much water do you use when you take a shower? Two gallons or more when you do that. How much when you flush your toilet? Is it one gallon, two gallons, three gallons? How much? Do you say thank you? Your body needs the water because you couldn't go to the bathroom if you don't have water."

I told all those hundreds of people, "We have to have you understand that your biggest concern for your life is water, giving thanks to it and thanking it every time you drink it, wherever you use it. So today I want you all to come up here and put your hand in this water and say, 'Forgive me, but from now on I will thank you wherever I use you.' Now, you all can do that. You're all not little tiny kids here. You're all up to where you can understand and pack this in your brain: if there's any water that you touch or come over—even when you're riding your car over a bridge or in an airplane—and you look out and see water, can't you say, 'Bless you' and 'Thank you'? I always do that when my car runs over a bridge. I say, 'Bless you, water, and all that live in you and all that drink from your bank. Bless you.' And I say, 'I really mean it, too.' I know the water can hear me. The water in my body can talk to the water out there. So, when you come up and touch the water today, the water inside can hear you."

I told them, "I have a medallion here from Dr. Masaru Emoto that shows how beautiful water looks when you treat it with love and compassion. So, when you talk to the water today, the water in your body is going to hear your words. And if you do this every morning for two weeks, I guarantee you that every one of you will feel better about your body, because you're talking truth to nobody but yourself." I told them, "Come up here now, children, babies, and all. Touch the water, you water babies, and thank it for your life. And tell it that you will think better about it every time you drink it or wherever you use it. You could do that. Do it every morning when you get up. Thank the Creator that He gave you another day, plus you can have a glass of water there and have a drink and say, 'Bless you for keeping me alive. Bless you for being in my body and in my tears and in my blood.' Learn to be grateful for the water. Just think of how long any of you could live without water. Maybe some of you already live where water is scarce. Just think about you not being able to have water right close by."

I asked them, "How many of you have the physical means to walk and get your water? How many of your relatives are unable to do that? Think about it. Do you have to get their water for them because they're crippled or bedridden or something? Even a person who has dementia has to have water. See to it that they get their water. A little baby has to have water instead of just milk. It is a precious thing, water. So, when you touch this water, you pray for it. Then the rest of the water that's left in this bowl, they'll take it back down with all your prayers in it, and it will go back into the Rhine River that we care about, the Rhine River here today. We want it to clear up, so this water that we're going to dump back in there with all your prayers is going to do that."

I asked them, "Do you believe me? Because it's true what I am telling you. The Creator said water can hear. The water can hear. The water that you're touching with all your prayers in it, that water will go back into the Rhine River and carry the message all through the water that is in the Rhine River. So, everybody, come on." They came up and touched the water. I said, "Babies and all, put their hands in it, and put some up on their forehead and bless them."

"So," I told them, "remember to thank the water. Tell it, 'Thank you for my life.' You can do that." So they all did. When we were through, I thanked everybody, babies and all. I said, "The babies won't hear me saying it, but when they get bigger, you can tell them that they were here and explain to them why. The water that you're dumping back in there now will give that message to the Rhine River that we care about it. And all of you live here, and sometime, when you're close to the water, walk by the shore and thank it for the pollution going away. Bless it. Talk to it. Some of you live right here by the Rhine River; I bet you could do that.

"No matter what river, no matter what well, no matter what ocean—anything that's water, talk to it and thank it; even the ocean needs our prayers because there's life in there, too. It's all part of the balance that we need for our lives in this world. It's our job; we are the ones that can carry the prayers for the planet and for the animal kingdom and all the swimmers in the water so that the water now will carry your message clear up through the Rhine River. And I thank everybody for participating today. And thank you, thank you, thank you. God bless each and every one and all your babies and everything.

"If you have family that wasn't here today, you teach them. I made you instant teachers, every one of you. Teach your neighbor. Teach your friend. Teach your enemy. Teach your community. Teach the elders that we're all water babies and that water is our first medicine. And I thank you all for joining me today. So now we wait and see what the message does to the river. Okay?" So, I thanked everybody.

Years later, there I am in Stockholm, Sweden, and here comes Dr. Barbara Smit—wonderful doctor; she treats herbally, and she has a lot of people that come to her. She came clear over and said to me, "I had to come, Grandma, because I want to tell you the salmon, the fish are back in the Rhine River." And this is about three and half years after we did all this blessing. Do you believe it? It's true. It's true. I was crying; my daughter was crying; we were all crying. How blessed that the Creator carried that message through the water and the water took it. All these messages from all these people went into that water, and I told them, "You know, being you're a water baby, the water will call you whether it is the ocean, a well, or the Rhine River. Wherever you are, the water will call you. So, give thanks to it for your life. Without it you can't live. Guard it with your life. Watch over it."

It is a human right, and I think water should be free to all humans, actually. I really do. I think that it should be available to everybody, that we shouldn't have to buy it. Especially in a plastic bottle, you know, because that's a cheap way for them to bottle it, and I think that's why they do it. They don't care if the water stays good in it. It's water. Whether the elements are still in there or not, it's not their concern once it goes into a store or a market or someplace for the consumer to get it. We're going to have to do a better job than we are doing about the water because most people are agnostic. They don't believe that water can hear. I know for a fact that the water could talk to the Cloud People. It's how you run this thinkin' thing. Do you believe? I never thought that I would get this old, going on ninety-one now, that I would have to buy water in a bottle. My god. It's scary, what is happening to our water everywhere. We need to think about the water in ourselves. Remember, water can hear. The water inside of you can talk to the water above you or the water in your glass. It might sound crazy, but it's true.

A long time ago I was called to the Everglades in Florida—a beautiful place. The Seminole Indians lived there. They never signed a treaty with the United States and still live in their *chickees*, their little round houses. There was big conglomerates drying up the swamp and filling it up and building condominiums, and it was angering the Seminole Indians, so they had me come down.

"Grandma, help us." So, I went down with Chief Billy to Fort Lauderdale. I told Chief Billy, "I bet this mayor was never sandwiched like this in his life between two Native Americans." Chief Billy spoke first, then the mayor, and then I spoke. We got up there, and we spoke about how we got to stop drying up the swamps. I said, "Those crocodiles and alligators being in canals? What are you thinking? They are not staying in there. They're crawling out and getting run over and getting in people's yards. They're not used to canals. It's got to stop." I said, "The people down there are frightened of what's happening to the swamp, and it has got to stay that way if you are all going to live around down there. It is part of the environment that you need for your life, so take care of it." To this day they have stopped that, and they have posted up signs taking care of the turtle. There are over-three-hundred-pound turtles. The rabbits are huge. The deer are just humongous.

When I went there, they had these huge, big hams above the fire, smoking 'em. Wonderful people that I got to stay with in their *chickees*, their houses. They used to be kinda open, but then they learned shame, so now they got boards around them, and they cover themselves up. The Indians down over in that country, too, are looking after their habitat. I have been all over Indian country telling people to guard the animal kingdom; watch over the habitat, be it on land or be it on water. There is more water base than there is land base, so you take care of the waters, too. It's important.

Even when I am flying in an airplane, and I look out the window and I see water, I bless it and thank it and all that live in it and all that drink from its shore. I bless it and thank it for giving life. I do that even when I am riding in my car over a bridge: "Bless you, water." I did that coming over here today, and all the water that I crossed to come over here, I thank the water. I do that ritualistically every morning. And I thank God because I have been at death's door many times in my life. When I wake up and the Creator gives me one more day, I am happy. One more day, we all can only do one day at a time. Make it a good one. But always think of your surroundings and where you live, what you could do to keep it good for our Mother Earth that has sustained us all up until this moment. All humans are water babies, born in water. And water is all of our medicine. So, think about it.

They took me to New York, got me on television and radio to talk about fracking. I said, "You're messing with that. Do you ever think if there is an action there is always a reaction? What's the reaction of what you're doing down there? You're going to screw up your water system. I guarantee you. Whether you believe me or not, keep on doing it and you'll understand what I am saying." They did screw up their water system. Anywhere they do that, they goof up the water system. I don't care where it is. They take off the tops of mountains for coal, then they take the coal out and they leave the rest, and the rains come and all the poisons and stuff come down the mountainside. Do they think of that? No. They don't care. It's the green frogskins they care about. It's nothing to do with life. It's always money.

Water is our first medicine. Guard it with your life. Without it we cannot live. We got to talk to the Cloud People, as I call them, because the Cloud People need to come and rain on the green so that the green can stay healthy so that we can breathe the good air. Like I say, when a tree breathes, I breathe. So remember that, water babies. Think of the water when you drink it, every day. When you wash your hands, take a shower, cook, wash your clothes, water your lawn, flush the toilet, wherever you use water. So it is a crucial thing, a needed thing, for all life. Use your voice to remember that the animal kingdom also needs water, and remember, we cannot live on this planet without the animal kingdom. Talk to the Cloud People, because you are all water babies.

Take care of the garbage. Put it in a good place. Like I used to teach my kids when they were little, you can't throw garbage out the car window because that's your Mother Earth out there. You would be throwing that on her face. There's always a place for garbage. My kids are all grandparents today, and they remember those words. So, teach your children that there's a place for garbage.

I will stop now, but I hope I have said something to get you to think about your environment, our environment, because our Creator said He has given us all everything that we need to live here, so use it like He said, in balance and moderation. Let's do a better job. Thank you ever so much. God bless you. Have a great day.

8

SACRED SALMON CEREMONY

I am sitting here today very grateful to be able to walk our planet, Mother Earth, and to speak about her and encourage people that we need to do a better job of taking care of our Earth Mother. We all care because we are all in this leaky canoe together. What can you do?

I was over in Crescent City when Spirit woke me and told me I had to go over here into Oregon and restore the Sacred Salmon Ceremony. I said, "You give it to someone else. I don't even live over there." But it kept coming, it kept coming, so my husband said, "Will you get something done and quit waking me up? You better just check out what you need to do." And I said, "Okay." This was in 1993.

I got ahold of a telephone book and I called around, and I found out that there was a forest service committee, the Star Ranger Station out over in Ruch, Oregon, over below the Applegate Dam on the Applegate River. I called them up and told them what Spirit wanted me to do. Spirit wanted me to restore the Salmon Ceremony that was done over there for thousands and thousands of years. So, they had us come over; first time two Indians sat on their committee. They asked me what I needed, and I said, "I need some land to restore the Salmon Ceremony that Spirit keeps telling me I have to do here on the Applegate River." I told them what I wanted to do and that my people had pit houses over here. They said yes, they do have the pit house. They asked me, "What do you want us to do about them?" I said, "Nothing. Just let the weeds grow up around them. It's alright, because they're still there." I said, "All I need is some land. I would like to bring back the ceremony that my people did over in the Applegate." So, they let me have seventeen acres in a place called Kanaka Flat down from Applegate Lake.

I started there, and in 1994 we came over, our truck loaded high with tables and chairs and benches and food that I had been gathering the whole year. We brought all of our cookin' sticks that were made out of the beautiful redwood. We use the redwood because when it's heated, there is no pitch in it to disflavor the fish. We had all our sticks and shovels and rakes and axes. We were loaded down. So we came over on the Applegate to Kanaka Flat to restore the Salmon Ceremony that the Creator said I had to do. I am pleased to say that my tribe jumped in there and helped; they got the fish for me.

We restored the Sacred Salmon Ceremony for the first time in the history of Southern Oregon. We renewed it in 1994, and in '95, here comes the State Fish and Game. They said, "Grandma, we don't know what you done, but there's more salmon in that river than we've ever heard of." I said, "Thank you." I said, "Well, when you teach reciprocity, then the Creator blesses." "What does that mean?" they asked. I said, "Well, to do the Salmon Ceremony, I do it like the Old Ones did for thousands of years. I had a sweat lodge put up and had it blessed—the covers, the willow, everything."

I told them that we have young divers doing what we call a *purification sweat*. We send the cedar boughs in there with them also, which are sacred to us. So, they're in there doing a purification sweat, and I have salmon cooked and give a taste to everybody there, elders down to the little people. I have a big beautiful fish bowl that they use to bring all the skin and bones back to me. Everybody, the little children and all, do that. When the divers come out of the purification sweat with the cedar boughs in their hands, I place the skin and bones on top of the boughs and then the drum starts. It drums the divers to the river. They stand on the river's edge, and they pray to the Salmon Nation.

I will just interject here that our people believe that salmon look like us two-leggeds but live in beautiful cities below the ocean floor. They choose every spring and every fall to come back and take the shape of salmon, because they live in such beautiful cities below the ocean floor. They come back and feed us at those times every year. So, we stand and give thanks to the Salmon Nation. Then the divers bring these bones and things back. They are sacred, and we love them. So they take these remains and put them back into fish. And then the divers dive in the cold water and put rocks on the bones and everything to hold them down, thanking the Salmon Nation and telling them how we love them, that they're sacred, and that we need them, as the divers pray under the water. Then the divers come back out. If it is a young man, and if he's a Native man, a young boy, he is a warrior now. So I give him an eagle feather. Then they all march around, and everybody there gets to honor them and hug them and thank them for what they have done for all of us. I told State Fish and Game that's what we teach in reciprocity, how to give back. That's what I've done at every Salmon Ceremony—teach reciprocity, how to give back to the Salmon Nation.

It is a special honoring thing that we do, and I am the only one; it's not done for everybody. It's not done in front of the public. It's quietly done in the evening, and I am the only one sittin' out there. It's not something to be shared publicly. It is a sacred thing. Eastman Kodak came one year and wanted to film the divers coming out of the sweat lodge, and I refused. So then they went away and wouldn't finish filming. Even the old men said no, no filming. It's so sacred that I am the only one sittin' out there when they take the remains to the river. It is a sacred thing.

When we did this above Gold Hill at a sacred place where we have what we call the "story chair," where they did the Salmon Ceremony there on the Rogue River for 22,000 years, I moved over there. I did that over there on Steve Keisling's property.

Steven calls his trailer house his tin can, and he said when he moved into that trailer he could feel some presence on that land. Well, then he got ahold of Thomas Doty, and Tom said, "We need to talk to Grandma." So then they give me a call, and I go over. This man that lived there, he said, "Grandma, what can we do about this presence?" I said, "I'll tell ya. My great-aunt Frances was a sister to Chief George Harney, my grandfather, and brought us all down to the river where the story chair was, where she told the stories of the people and the languages, the skirmishes and the battles." I brought a picture of my father sitting in that story chair. That picture was taken by John P. Harrington, the archeologist that lived in our home in 1935. Thomas Doty and them were looking for it, couldn't find it for many years. Then I come up with the picture, and he hit me on the head and said, "You been holding out on us." I said, "I didn't know anybody was lookin' for it."

So here I am over there with them, with this picture that they were looking for of my dad sittin' in that story chair. Then I told them about how my people came to that spot, sat up there in that story chair looking down at this big pool where somebody would watch the salmon come. Was it time to start the Salmon Ceremony? The word would spread out all over. All the Native people would come, and they'd start catchin' fish, and they'd have their big Salmon Ceremony. That was the presence that Steve was feeling on this property. I said, "The only way to appease it and make you feel good is I could bring the Salmon Ceremony back. My people did it right here for 22,000 years." So, I did. I brought it back.

There was a dam there called Powerhouse Dam, and I didn't like the name of the Powerhouse Dam. I didn't like that. That had to come down. So, we did some sort of yakkity-yakking around about it and praying about it, and finally it came down. I was standing on the bank crying when that dam came down, when the big trucks were there taking the big cement blocks that they tore down and hauled away. I renamed it Tillamook Falls, which is today on the map, and there is a sign out on the highway called

Tillamook Falls. I am very honored because my people are the people of the river, and that is what Tillamook means, "People of the River."

So, here I am. I come back. Then I wanted to go sit down there for quite a few years. When that opportunity came about, I talked to Steve and them, and Roger got it all rigged up, and I got to go and sit in that chair. My family, they were so upset that I was going to go down in this boat down there and sit in this chair in class-five rapids—pretty rough. Oh god, my kids were mad. They didn't want me going down there. I said, "God, you kids. I can swim." Well, that didn't matter to them. My daughter had even called my doctor and told him what I was doing. He said absolutely not, but that didn't help. But also—which was scary for my kids—was the day before. Us International Grandmothers have a very special photographer for us—her name is Marisol Villanueva—and she came clear from New York and filmed me all through the Salmon Ceremony. And they said they'll take her down on a special run. So they took her down the day before I went, and low and behold, two guys fell out, and that didn't help my family. They were all the more riled up. Standing there, they did everything but hit me with one of those sticks. They were really up in arms for me not to do this. I said, "Don't worry about it. I can swim." "Yeah, but you got those buckskins on." I had my $10,000 buckskin dress on, $2,000 beaded basket cap, and my boot moccasins. They took off my boot moccasins, and my kids were standing there, and they did everything but put a rope on me to pull me out of the boat.

The Nike people came from out in Hillsboro, Oregon, and brought me Nike tennis shoes. They took off my moccasins and put these Nike shoes on. It was hilarious. Nike shoes with a buckskin dress. Then I had my beaded cap on, and they put a helmet over that, and over the top of my dress was this great big hunk of plastic. In the boat with me was Oliver Fix, the world's gold medalist kayaker; his wife, Gilda, who is also a world-class rafter; and Steven Keisling, an Olympic rower, whose land and boat we were in. I thought, nothing is going to happen to me with these guys in there, so I didn't have any qualms about going down the river.

There was two men already taken down there earlier. They pulled me out and took me up there. I was excited that I got to go down there where my dad sat all those years ago. They pulled me up out of the raft, and I got to sit where my dad sat in 1935. I had my eagle feather with me, and you could see it in the pictures that were taken. So I was sittin' up there on that rock. I was crying and holding up my eagle fan, looking up and telling my dad, "Here I am, Dad. I come full circle. And I am sitting where you sat, and I pray that you watch over me, all of you up there." Where I sat is where all the Indians sat when they came there and did their Salmon Ceremony.

There's a big eddy down below that big rock where that chair is, and there they can see the fish, and they knew when to be able to do the Salmon Ceremony. They had people as a lookout watching for the salmon, and when the salmon came, then they'd set up this big gathering. People would come from all over Southern Oregon and everywhere. It was such a peaceful thing. And this man that owned the lands said he could feel it on his land and said to me, "What am I going to do about it, Grandma? Is there anything?" And I said, "That's what I am going to do. I will restore the Salmon Ceremony over here." And I did, so it has been a good thing.

Now I am going to put the Dragonfly Bridge close to that place. The main thing behind all of this was that there was all these dams on the rivers and streams of Southern Oregon, and I had walked around the Savage Rapids Dam close to Grants Pass, close to where I lived years back when I could get around better. I saw all of the garbage and the debris piled high behind that dam, and I thought, oh dear god, what a mess. So then I walked around the riparian zone and the edges of the river and I saw algae building up. I knew that once you have algae, next comes the mercury. I told the commissioners a long time ago, "Do we wait until something dies or someone dies before something is done about that dam? It's a mess." I said, "I've been up along all the rest of them, too, and they're all a mess. They been there for over ninety years. What good are they?" So the city began to get money to take the dam down. There it is, all these years now— two years ago, all the dams are off the rivers, all the way in South- ern Oregon. There was a lot of people that walked with me, that prayed with me that this could happen. I attribute so much of this to them and their trustworthiness, and their stick-to-it-ness with me all those years.

I used to cook way down in Hollywood. My son Keith was with me, and my son Tony Jr. Kay Starr and her husband, and a big guy—his name was Jay Silverheels—and his wife Mary, and some of the other Hollywood stars would come around, and I would cook down there. They would call me up in Crescent City and say, "How deep do we dig the pit to put the meat in? What can we use to marinate the meat in?" And then I would say, "Go down to the store and get a new garbage can, and put in all the stuff that I tell 'em to marinate the meat in. And get some foil." Then, after they got the meat all marinated and everything, it was how to put the spices. So, we put bay leaf, garlic, and other stuff, and I would marinate it in those new garbage cans. I said, "When it's marinated, you roll it in the foil, and then you go down and you buy some new gunnysacks and get some wire. So you take and roll the meat in the foil, and then you take and roll it in a new gunnysack and twist it at the ends and put the bale over the top so that they can lift it out with a pitchfork or a rake. Then put a slant in the bottom of the pit." "What kind of wood do we use?" "Well, you're down there with orchards. You got apples. Apple trees will work. If you have some old apple trees, use that. So, okay, then we put it all in there." I said, "The steaks that are rare, the roast go down first, and then up above that is the steaks that come out more rare. Put those bales on it so you can lift 'em up, okay?" "What are we going to cover it with?" I said, "Go get some corrugated roofing, and then the dirt that you have piled over there, get some wheelbarrows, haul it over and put it over the top after you get the fire going in it. Build it up good. Heat the rocks good that you're going to put at the bottom and then put the corrugated roofing and the dirt over the top of that. If you see steam coming through, get the shovel and put it on top where the steam is comin'."

Then I got the girls from Morongo Indian School 'cross over on the res to come over, do the fry bread. They did a good job. It was great. Woody Gunther and Kay Starr's husband, they just got in there and worked with us. I was this talker over it all, raising funds for young Indian kids to have a scholarship. It went off great. Jonathan Winters—that's who I was trying to think of— Jonathan Winters is a crazy guy, nice guy, and anyway, we're right down there in Moore Park in Hollywood, cookin' in the back of Ernie Ford's home. Dorothy Lamour was going to come over. She was across the street, but she got in an accident a few days before, so she was stuck in her bed, but she sent word over. Anyway, there we are; we did our cooking and everything, raising funds for scholarships for First Nation students. That's what we were doing. Jay Silverheels was there to talk to, a lot of fun. But they filled it all back in later. They had all the dirt piled back. But it was generous of him and a generous heart to let us do that.

I was called from Eugene, Oregon, one year if I could cook for the Calvinistic Confederation of the United States and Canada. "Sure" flew out of my mouth, and I thought, god, what have I done, I don't know. But anyway, where we had to go was south of Florence, Oregon, way out in the middle of nowhere, close to the ocean. I had to hire people to come in and mow the grass. I got my wood from Toledo. I got my big water tanks from Corvallis. I got my fish from Charleston, Oregon. I had all my tables lined up, and I had all my young people of my tribe. I had young boys standing down there to put the wood in when the cooks say they need some wood. I taught them how to lay it. Here we are at the first table, and there's a guy just standing there to put one fish up. That man takes off all the fins and makes sure it's all clean inside. He sends it up to the next guy, who filets it out and puts the head in a place, and the tail goes in another place, and then it goes on up.

The slabs go up to somebody else who cuts 'em in pieces. Then it goes on up into a pan, and then those people down there put the salt, the pepper, the garlic, and then it goes on down the line. Then I have some people standing down there that slide them on the sticks one piece at a time. I taught them how the belly part goes up first and then the fatter part down the bottom of the stick. Then I had two boys at the end to take those sticks over to the cooks that we had with big twenty-five-foot pits built with sand—big berms on the side—and then I had to stand there and make sure that the sticks go through all of it, because if you're cooking, you can't be messin' 'round trying to find a place to put the stick. So I had one end fixed for when they got cooked. You could set them back on this place here that had to be nice—no rocks, no sticks or nothing in it.

That was the way the assembly went. Then I had people to take them off the sticks, put 'em in pans to be served, and then I had people down the other end of the table to where they could take a knife and use the back of the knife upside down to scrape the fish off of the sticks and take a wire grill to rub them down to make the stick okay again, to start again. I had nine busloads come in first to feed, and I said, "Two hours later bring in nine more." That would give us time to have the sticks clean, the fish back on, cooked, and back out again. It worked like clockwork. It went off really great. People didn't think I could do it, but I said, "We can do it. We can do it." And so they listened to me, everybody.

My cooks—I got some of the best Yurok cooks on the river, which is my husband and his buddy. I just went to a funeral the other day, and Merkey Oliver and his wife and all of them came up to help me cook. I paid them all handsomely, too. Cooked all over down through that country, my husband and I. We have cooked for a lot of people, and I cooked at the White House. Went to the White House and there was lines of people, and they had to—what kind of wood? It was apple alder, and they had madrone, that kind of wood for our fire. All these people were lined up hours before the fish came off, and they wanted a sample of it. I sent a stick with fish on it into the White House. Was the first time they ever heard of it, and I got to do that. It really went off really good.

It was a festival that they were going to have, and people heard of me down through Hollywood way; word got around. So, when I got back there, they first got us some fish that was so thin that I said, "This ain't gonna work." They had to reorder clear back to the Klamath River. They had some of the fishermen there, and I forgot who then came up with the fish. Anyway, they had to send me some more fish that would stay on the stick. It had to have enough meat on it to stay on the stick.

I took my sticks with me. And I commend my children because they were all my cooks every year, and my great-grandchildren, and my great-greats, they all helped me. Without you all this couldn't have been done, so I owe you a tremendous thing, all of you, my love. I sure thank each and every one of you from the youngest to the oldest. God bless you kids. You know you made good medicine for yourself so that when I am gone you can still do this if you wish. You know how to do it, and you are good, all of you. I never hear you complain. I'd ride around and watch and see if something was being neglected, or fish getting burnt, or sticks getting burnt. You guys are good.

I didn't have to go and say, "Hey, turn this, take that off, and have to go up there," and screech around at you. I didn't have to do that. So bless you all. You did such a beautiful job, it's great. I thank you. There was a lot of people now that I have done twenty-one years, and I said, "I can quit now." But there's a lot of elders that have called me in the last year, and a bunch saying, "Are you going to have another Salmon Ceremony, Grandma? Because we look forward to it. You are the only group here in a year's time that we can go and be comfortable in, because you don't have alcohol or drugs around." And I said, "Oh, I can't do it anymore. Twenty-one years now, we've accomplished a lot. We got people watching for garbage on the rivers because rivers are not garbage dumps." So, I've been workin' with people all those years to stop the garbage on the rivers and streams. I pray that they will continue to do that. If you live on top of the river bank, please, where you live, don't be throwing things in it, because there's life in that water, and it's our obligation to be a voice and to take care of the habitat of the rivers and streams. There's life in those waters. Not just our rivers and streams, but our ocean, too.

It is our job as human beings to look after these things. You are that voice. You are the voice for the voiceless, and they only have us for a voice, remember? So, I pray that the legacy that I will leave to all of you will make you instant teachers, and then you continue on to your children, and your children's children, so the message goes on and on. You teach what I have taught you.

9

EARTH MOTHER,
ANIMALS, AND FOOD

We have to learn to do things in moderation and balance. We have to learn that. When Spirit came to me a long time ago and told me I was going to walk the spiritual path, I told Him, "No, I am not. Give it to somebody else. I am not worthy. I am not good enough. I have done this, this, and this—no." But anyway, I have finally accepted it. There is that walk that we all have to do, whether it's you, whether it's me, that we have an obligation to Earth Mother to do a better job than we're doin'. For instance, I think if there's trees to be cut, it should be selective instead of clearcutting. I have fought for this on television and everything way back there, that we got to stop making the roads up there. Then, when there is clear-cuts, they don't put the roads to bed. Then we end up with erosion, year after year after year. When is it going to stop? Some of those loggers and some of those logging companies must have grandchildren. Don't they think of them? What are they going to have to live through of what they're doin? You know? There's got to be a better way of makin' paper. You know, we all need it, we know that. But there has got to be a better way of taking care of the trees; I don't go with clearcut because of the erosion, you know, and the waste, and the roads. We have a lot of rain here in Oregon. There is a lot of erosion when they leave things like that. It is not fair to me, it is not fair to you, it is not fair to the littlest child. It is not fair.

My dad was one of the top loggers in the country a long time ago, and he taught my brothers logging. It was more money in that in those days. They all learned. My dad was a tough logger. Nobody would fight with my dad, either, and when my brothers go up, nobody messed with my brothers. When we learned to box, nobody messed with us girls. Anyway, the logging was there. They had to make money. That was the only way that the males could go out and make a living was through logging. What are we down to now? Two percent of the trees in the world? I have even been fighting for big trees in South America because there's so much habitat in every tree. There's a least five in every tree. And not only in the tree—below the tree, where it makes shade for something else down here. And to cut those big trees down, just think of the erosion. Think of the water supply and what it's going to do to the people. To me it's scary. It is really scary. So, I am always praying for those people down there in South America. "Grandfather, help them. Manifest yourself to them some way to salvage their water. They need it so badly." I am praying right now that they are talking about recycling water in Southern California already, and it is coming, this water world that I am talking about. And plastic isn't good for ya. The elements of stuff going through the plastic, and it's not good for the water.

There's people over there at Humboldt State and all those students over there banning the plastic bottle—bottled water. I had a Southern Oregon University thermos over there, and they commended it. Even Grandma has a good bottle. Then it got to leakin' the other day, so I had to get another one. But anyway, I've been fighting the plastic. They're fighting the plastic bags over there. Getting all of those students over there, wherever they live, to help spread the word—stop the plastic—because it's sad of all the plastic that is flying around out there. I am always concerned.

You know, a long time ago they flew me around all over Oregon and along the coast clear up into Alaska to show me about clearcut logging. I was probably forty-five or fifty years old then, and it scared me. It should scare everybody because it is not right what is happening. We might need paper, but we don't need to be taking the tops off the mountains. We don't need to be clearcut logging.

I think there is such a thing as selective logging. Also, when the logging companies build the roads up in the mountains, they don't put them to bed when they're done. And that erosion comes down the mountainside into our rivers and streams. It's not good for all the swimmers in the water, either. So I hope that when you start taking the trees down that you think about our rainforest and help to maintain the delicate system of interdependent plants and animals and bacteria. They all play an important part in the climate of our planet.

Rainforests around the world are being subjected to deforestation, which is affecting—often eliminating—the homes of many animals. I am going to tell you about some of them that are affected: The alligator, the anaconda, the ant eater, the army ants, the lizard basilisk, the beetle, the kangaroo. It's the fish, the catfish, crab, the crocodile, the parrot, the salamander, the slough, the tapir, the eagle—even our national bird—the gorilla, the harpy—which is a bird—and the jaguar, the lemur, the macaw—that's the parrot—the mantis, the margay, the monkey, the ocelot, the orangutan, the pacu—the fish—the tarantula, and the termite, and the toucan. Now, you might not have a lot of these animals around where you are, but I always tell people, even the people of the cloth, ministers and priests, that they should stand up, when they give prayers, to pray for the existence of these things that got a right to live.

My god, they are part of a balance for all of us around the globe. It's bad here in the state of Oregon where I sit today. About five, six years ago there was about two hundred species of wildlife that is gone—kaput. We only will be able to see them or read about them in a book. Now, if you do like I do and multiply that by the rest of our states, to me it's frightening. It's our job as human beings to keep the balance and to watch out for the habitat of all life, because the animal kingdom is put here for our existence. We cannot live on this planet without them. I put this list together, and when I looked at it, I just shuddered to think that we're losing the habitat of all these things.

Now I've been working for thirteen years, and what has been gone is the condor. I have been working hard with the Portland Zoo people to bring the condors home because they're part of our balance here in the state of Oregon. I pray that people are listening to me and will help me with that. There were only twenty-two left in the world, and they were flying the blue skies here in Oregon. Over thirteen years ago David Moen and his buddy Mike said, "Did you see the condors when you were little, Grandma?" I said, "No, I don't remember, but my dad said they were here. They were here when I was a little kid. When I was a little girl, my dad said they called them the thunderbird and they were here, part of the balance." So these guys, to verify what I said, crawled all over the mountains in Oregon to validate that. They found evidence. From that time on, I have been workin' with the condors to bring them back so they can fly our beautiful skies in Oregon, because they're a part of the balance here.

I am fighting all the time to try to bring home the condors. I am trying to get everybody to help me to get the lead out of bullets. We could use other things like steel or copper, something that is just as effective as lead. But if we bring home the condors and then the hunters out there shoot a deer, for example, and clean the deer out there and leave the insides, and the condors come along and eat it, they're going to get lead poisoning. It's not right. I have been working for thirteen years to bring the condors back to the state of Oregon. I have been working all these years with the people from the Portland Zoo to bring the condors back to Oregon. Now I have got pamphlets and stuff with me that tell you about the lead poisoning. If a female condor gets lead poisoning, when she lays her eggs, the shells are so soft that they will not hatch. And she slowly paralyzes inside and dies. A few years back, there was only twenty-two condors here in the world. Now there are over four hundred. So stand with me and be a voice to stop the lead in the bullets so we can bring the condors back to Oregon. We can do that. Help their life. I pray that you could do that. Let's talk to the hunters and help them to join us so that the condors can fly over our heads again.

I think it's a wonderful thing when they were bringing them back in Oregon out of a little place called Carver, just a little ways from Portland. They had me to come up and bless the nest. They hadn't yet put condors in it, so I am going to go all over out there where they put some big trees up, go inside the nest for them to be able to fly a little bit and land up there. Then they had a big building where they had the nesting area. They had about a foot of sand for the female to lay her eggs to hatch in the sand. Then they had a place for the roosting area. They connected it with a big wooden ledge. Well, the condors wouldn't fly in it when they did come because they had to make that ledge look like a rock. So they did that. That afternoon, after I got through blessing the compound, they brought back two pair, and they were pecking on my cane, the guys. So now I have been with them, and they had me to come up to Portland again to bless thirty-nine of them. Who has seen that many condors? My daughter Nadine was crying. I was crying. My heart was so full to be able to see these big, majestic birds all sitting around out there on their roosts, and to pray that the Creator would bless us and let them come home. I am working now down to Big Sur, California, at the nesting grounds, to pray for them down there. I have been involved all these years, and I've been back up to Portland and had other tribal people to come and help us. So, you too, reading this—you too, stop using the lead so we won't be killing off the condors when they come home. I am sure you can do that. I am sure. Please do it, not for just the children that are here on this earth right now, but for those that are seven generations of the unborn.

I am going to approach my tribe, because I have the paperwork now that we can give out to people, the effects that this is having on the condors. So I pray that you, too, can help me, that

we can see the condors and watch after them when they come
back here to our state. Please join me in watching out for their
habitat. I even opened for the Yurok Portland Summit, so now
they got two birds back in Northern California, and I am very
proud that they got to go back. The people down there have been
workin' hard to understand about the condors and about their
nesting places and all of it. I am very proud about that because
they, too, haven't been able to sing their condor song at the earth
renewal dances because they didn't have the condors. I pray now
that they are going to be there forever for the balance in California. They, too, know about the lead in bullets and are trying hard
to get hunters and even the young kids that have .22s and stuff to
buy bullets that don't have any lead in it.

I started the Sacred Salmon Ceremony in '94, bcause I see all
the garbage that is in the rivers, the dams here piled high with
garbage, and it wasn't good for anything. So here I have done
twenty-one years now, and the dams are all off the rivers and the
salmon are able to swim free for the first time in ninety years.
A lot of people helped me with that, and I give them credit for
standing with me and supporting me on these things. So we, as
the two-leggeds, have an obligation to take care of the habitat of
all of these things. All the animals that we have here, we couldn't
live without them. When you pray, include them in your prayers.
And stop the garbage. You know, that's our job, and I believe we
have hurricanes and tornadoes and all those waters washing up on
the lands around the world killing people because we're not grateful. We don't thank the water for anything, and it's sad because we
need to do that. You can pray for the water and be thankful for it.

Learn to pray for the animals, too, that live around here in
Oregon. It is our job as human beings to look after them. I pray
that you can do what you can to help save the habitat. Save the
wolf that's come home, wolf OR-7, and his family. He's part of
the balance here, too. Don't be shooting 'em. They have a job
here, too. I pray that those of you that know how to pray, pray for
all these things of the animal kingdom. I pray that you will listen

to all of these things that I have been saying about the loss of the habitat and some of these animals and birds that are going to be extinct. The only place we'll be able to see them is in a book. So, thank you so much.

And another thing: look at what you're buying. Are you buying too much stuff with salt in it? You better check it out. Are you eating right? There, again, my great-grandmother—people asked her what did she attribute her longevity to, living so long? And she said, "I babied my stomach." I didn't know what that meant when I was young and heard her say it, but as I grew up, I found out that it's important what goes down your mouth—how you live your life.

Do a good thing. Make sure that your system is getting enough of the good stuff. They always got labels and organic things in grocery stores. Make sure you're buying organic because that GMO stuff should be banned. A long time ago when they were talking about this GMO thing I thought, *oh*. It came to me from the spirit world that these imitation seeds—Spirit said that they have to make special fertilizer for it. Oh, I thought, I live in Oregon where it rains a lot, and if a farmer plants these GMO seeds and the rains come and wash off these chemicals on their fertilizer, it is going to get in our rivers and streams, and it is not right. It is not right for that. Or the wind is going to blow, and blow some of this over into the next farm. It is going to contaminate. Use your voice to try to stop these things. I have an adopted son that has Agent Orange, and he was in the war in Vietnam, and he got this Agent Orange. He is suffering to this day with his body, and that was manufactured by GMO. So, you think about the GMO stuff like I do. When I go shopping, I make sure that the food that's going down my mouth and into my stomach is the good stuff. I think that you have an obligation to yourself to read your labels. Watch out for the salt, especially if you're older. You don't need all that salt. I use a little Himalayan salt. The sweetener I use is stevia, if I use any sweetener, and I use it sparingly.

If I can do this, you can too. I pray that you watch how you're shopping so that you can teach your children the way to shop and read the labels. Make sure it is the good stuff in 'em. I hope I have said something today to encourage you and to help you to look after your family and yourself. You have an obligation to yourself to eat right, the fruits and the vegetables. I used to tease my sons that were kind of young and didn't want to eat salads. They said, "Oh, this stuff is rabbit food," and I said, "Rabbits don't have glasses, so you kids better eat your vegetables." They began to eat their vegetables. My kids today are all grandparents, and they eat good. They're all good cooks. I have a son that's left. He is a good cook. He is seventy years old. I lost his brother, my oldest son, and my youngest son, who has gone on with the beloved Creator. They're in a better place than I am, so that's okay. It won't be long, I'll join them. I hope not for another ten, fifteen years though, because I have things to do, as I tell my beloved Creator.

My kids, all of them, they are eating good. My son is over-weight, and I told him the other day—I was over there with him—that he better start watchin' what's goin' down his mouth, and he better start makin' sure that he loses some weight because, I said, it is going to hinder your life. I pray that he listens to me, and I pray today that you have an obligation to how you run your life. I hope I have said something that will encourage you to watch what you're doing, watch every step you take. People, elders even, have asked me how I do it. I am going on ninety-one. I said, "It's easy, one foot in front of the other. You just got to keep on moving." I say, how you run your head, you run your body that way. So do a good job. You only got from the time you get up in the morning to the time you lay your head down at night, just that many hours. Another thing the Creator told me a long time ago: He has given all us humans everything we need down here on this earth to survive. Take care of it and use it in moderation and balance. Here we are, we've walked away from that, and we've got a hole in the ozone layer, and we got smog in our cities. We got pollution in our rivers and streams and oceans, so listen to me. Let's do a better job so that your grandchildren's grand-children's grandchildren can have good air, good water. I work hard so that my generation of children, the fifth generation, can grow up and be grey-headed like me and have good air and good water.

I bless you all for learning. I hope I have said something to encourage you, to strengthen you, to help you on your path, because nobody could do your life but yourself. How you do it? Easy. One foot in front of the other. So keep it movin'. Do it the best you know how, with gratitude and love. Thank you, thank you, thank you.

10
MY TOTEMS

They somehow carry a message of my totems. It's amazing. They all seem to give me a blessing. My tribe did the reversal of the Trail of Tears from Siletz, Oregon, down the coast to Gold Beach, thirty miles up the mountain to Agnes. I was up there in my car. I was the oldest grandmother there to greet the runners. They called me way down, ten miles down, and said they were needing prayers. So, word came up for me to pray, and I said, "I'll pray." I got out of my car, and I stood out and prayed and sent energy to the runners. I said, "Grandfather, you take care of the runners. They got good legs. I wish I could do that. I would be there with them. So, you take care of them and let them come on in and help them." I did quite a lengthy prayer for them, got back in my car, and drove back up to where they're going to come up. I was sittin' there when they all got there, and I was the first elder to greet the runners.

This is the first time they did the run in reverse of the Trail of Tears of my people up there. When they did it, I was behind them, and I thought I better not crowd them because they were going down under a little knoll, down under the trees, where they had tables set up for them to eat. So, I thought, I will just pull off here and wait till they get down there, then I will drive down. I pulled up and shut off the key, and I looked up in my windshield, and my mouth flew open like a hippo. It was all covered in dragonflies. I put my head down on the steering wheel and cried and thanked the Creator. "Thank you, bless you, bless you for my people and what they're doing. Touch them and help them." I was praying, "Thank you, beloved Creator, for the messengers, that we're doing the right thing for our people that have gone on, and that you have them up there. Let them know that we feel honored for them sending the messengers, the dragonflies, to show that they are watching and that they are aware of what we have done, our people here, in honor to the ancient ones." I never saw anything like it. It's a phenomenal thing. I felt really good to be able to tell that story to all of them down there when we had lunch.

I got an iron dragonfly door knocker. I've got them all around my picture frames, in my pillows, in my socks, in my aprons, in my purses, in my jewelry, hanging from my trees, everywhere in my house. There's many things about how the dragonfly has been in my life and what it means. It's everywhere, and it's phenomenal how it's come; my people said when they died and went to the Star Nation, they came back as dragonflies. So, all of these that have come to me over the years warms my heart. I've got them in pins, and stuff in my hair, and in my abalone, and everything. It always seems like no matter what that dragonfly's shape or what kind of material, they all seem to give me a blessing. It is amazing. This necklace, like this one that come with me today—I've got all kinds of beaded ones. This one wanted to come.

I always believed that just because the dragonflies are bead-work and stuff, they still somehow carry a message. I got them in my caps. A certain one wants to ride or be with me or on my arm. It flashes in my head, so I say, "Okay, I'll take ya." Or my earrings; sometimes I will take them and want to wear one of them. It's phenomenal how these things have come like that in my totems. Like when I am really tired and how that bear medicine comes through. I think, god, I just can't stay up another minute, but I do. So I attribute it to—it comes from the bear power. Same way with the eagle. It's a messenger. Long before Congress made it the national bird for us, our Native people throughout the land had already had the eagle that way because he could fly the highest and see the farthest and carry our messages to the Beloved. It was already one of our totems. I gathered that when the eagle comes to different places that I am driving or something and they come swooping down over me. My daughter, it just shakes her up because it's going right over the top of us. I said, "Good. It's with us."

Messengers. I acknowledge the messengers of our beloved Creator in so much of where I journey. I don't care what country it is in. Just like when we were down at Montezuma Wells, all of us riding along: "Grandfather, where is the messenger? Am I doing the right thing here?" Pretty soon I look out and poked my daughter, "Look, look!" Right close to the window, a big ol' hawk flying around. "Oh, thank you, Grandfather." Pretty soon it goes away. Pretty soon here it comes again. Whoa! It's unusual. You know it's unusual, but you know that the Creator let me know that we're in the right place, doing the right thing. Like when they dedicated this mountain up here after me. Five eagles up there. Bless you, Grandfather. Whoa! That's great. Then the drag-onflies over my head. I am in the right thing, tellin' everybody, "You know, we're doing a good thing here." It is a validation to me, just like coming over here. "Grandfather, send me a messenger big bird over there, a great big red-tailed hawk. Thank you!" You know that I am being blessed and what I am supposed to do here today. Don't question it. Don't say, "Awe, that bird couldn't be sittin' out there for me." I don't do that. It was there so I took that medicine and put it in here and said, "Thank you for the validation, Grandfather."

Over a year ago I had a vision. It just really startled me. I said I've been all over the world and never heard of such a thing as a dragonfly bridge. What Spirit told me is, "You are going to build this dragonfly bridge, a walk bridge across the river, and when you put the bridge across, you are going to put three pillars underneath on both sides of the bridge. Don't put those pillars where they will interfere with the rookery up there where birds have been coming for hundreds of years. Don't put the pillars down where they will be close to the spiritual storage here that's down the river. Don't put it next to that. When you build a bridge across, you are going to have to put some mesh up there to keep the people from jumpin' over and getting hurt or drowning." Spirit said, "When you put the mesh up, you put the long, huge dragonfly wings embedded on that mesh. Inside of the big dragonfly wings you put the different colors of all the dragonflies interspersed, if you wish, with salmon jumping. You put those small ones inside of the big wings of the dragonfly wings that you put up. Then you make some that will light up at night for those that walk across it at night. Then you put a monument on each end of the bridge explaining about the dragonfly, how my old people said when they left this earth and went to the Star Nation that they came back as dragonflies." They called them the Daldal. Spirit said, "So, you put that on the bridge, and that will explain about why the dragonfly bridge is there." When I saw that I thought, dear me, I've been all over the world, I've never heard of such a thing as a dragonfly bridge. But I never worried and thought anymore about it, and I just let it go. Until not too many months ago a man came to my house and said that Gold Hill wanted to put a walk bridge across the river. "Oh," I said, "I saw that." "What did you see, Grandma?" And I explained about my vision and that I saw the dragonfly bridge. The next thing I knew, about three weeks after he came, there was an artist that came from Port Angeles, Washington, to draw out my vision.

I went through it all again with him and he drew it all out. What he drew out went to the Gold Hill City Council. They had me come back over it, and they accepted it. Channel 12 was there, and they had me on Channel 12 talking about the dragonfly bridge. So, I feel good in my heart that I got to see that. At the end of the bridge, the monument explained how my people said that when they died and they went to the Star Nation, they all came back as dragonflies. So, dragonflies have been a phenomenal thing in my life. Like when they named the mountain up over here at Ashland Taowhywee Peak, there was dragonflies all over my head, and five eagles. There was a lot of people up there that were witnessing all of this. Every place I have been around the world—I have traveled a lot—the dragonflies always come. I always say it is the Creator's messengers.

The dragonflies have been all over and hanging out in my trees. They have been a messenger to me, and I don't need to know which one is which, it's just that I know that I've been blessed when they come around and I see them like this. It's been a great thing, and I teach this to many people about the dragonflies, to honor them because they, too, can be like a totem to anybody. They have been my totem ever since I was a little kid, always coming to me until I found out why they did. I feel so honored to be able to say that today the ancient ones can cross the veil and come to me through these messengers of the Creator—and the eagle, and the hawk, and the dragonfly. I always say that that's the Creator's messengers coming over here. There's one or two always sittin' out where I can see them.

I always feel like I have been honored and I am doing the right thing in my everyday life. I hope that when you see a dragonfly—maybe it's your ancestors—that you can honor them by sayin' a prayer to them, because all of those Old Ones that stand behind all of us, it took 'em all to make us who we are. So, if you pray, pray and thank them for who you are. They are all inside of you. I always say that the Old Ones of this land are always behind me, nudging me and letting me know that they're aware of my walk and that they can be a part of my life, and they keep on encouraging me. They do that a lot. The dragonfly maybe could be a messenger to you also. I thank you for being able to understand that this is just not me that could have these dragonflies around. They can come to you, too, because all of us have ancient ones that have gone on, and they're up there too. Thank you for listening. God bless you, and have a great day.

11

SPIRIT-DRIVEN

A lot of people said "You shouldn't be driving. You're ninety years old." I said, "So? My car don't know that." I always drive in my car, but I am not alone. I have the Creator with me. I thank my Beloved to be with me and guide me and keep me safe in my car and take care of it from the tires up. I am confident that my sky pilot works for me and is with me all the time. So if yours don't work, you can borrow mine. I feel it is spirit-driven. I feel that. I look at it as a must. A must thing that has to be heard and that other people can adopt and use. It can benefit others. Somebody is going to say, "Ah, I wish I would have thought of that," or, "I am not too late. I can do this with my child," or, "I want to take care of Grandma, because she's the wisdom-keeper in our family."

Love is the whole thing behind everything. All of this I've done is because I love, because I care. I think that we need to impress that onto grandfathers, dads, moms, and families, make them sit in that chair and look at themselves; that's what I'd like to see them do. Put yourself in that chair and take a look at yourself. Can you do it better? Always there's a way to do something better. Is it too late? No. It's never too late. If you could just say to your child, "I love you." Like my kids—there's never a time that they don't call and say, "I love you, Mother," or "I miss you, Mom." My daughter, she never goes to her room—when we're together or wherever we are, she says, "I love you, Mom." And it's great, because she's had two heart attacks and I always think, Grandfather, don't you dare have her have something happen in the night and I have to get up and go in there and help her. Don't do that to me or to her. I need her, Grandfather. I am living this long, doing your work that you put me on this path to do, so you keep me goin', and you take care of her, too."

I think that the love that I have in my heart for you people, you're a part of me because you're that extension of me. I am really proud to be able to do this for the world out there, because I am saying, "Wake up, America. Wake up a family. Wake up a grandmother. Wake up a grandfather. Wake up Mom, Dad, a child, a teacher." A teacher is a parent away from home. A kind word to a kid, like my grandson, who is the youth ambassador to us Grandmas, like, "You know what, Grandson, I am so proud." And he hugs me, great big guy. And we are proud of him. I tell him, "We hear from others that you're around up there how you're doin'. We don't have to call you, they tell us. I am proud of the words that are coming about you." I thank the Creator for him and all my grandchildren and my granddaughters. One of them was in prison. She turned her life around. I said, "Don't mention it to me. It's already forgiven. Don't mention it to yourself. It's all forgiven. You're on a good path now, and we don't have to fuss about you anymore."

It's that way with my children. When I talk to my baby girl that's up there near Salem, the first words are, "I love you, honey. I just called, checkin' in. Lettin' you know how things are down here and where I am goin'." I do that. It don't take but a little bit of time, and it means a lot to my children. So, I do that. I check in with them all the time. And if I need to call, I can pray and nudge that kid to have to call me. "What do you want?" My son, he's seventy years old, he says, "Mom can sure wrestle to be around without even calling." I just pray. The Creator does long-distance healing for my children. I don't have to be right there. I know my Creator can take care of them. Every day I sit in the morning and pray for all my family.

I am the only one left of my kids. My brothers and sisters, too, are all gone. Some of their kids call me Auntie Grandma. I love it. Every day I am thanking my brother and my Creator for my brother's and sister's kids, that He is taking care of them. "Breathe your healing breath into those that need you, Grandfather, for my brother's and sister's children." Know that those up above know that I do that. So, the medicine goes all around. I don't have to say, "Did you do it?" I hear later that things are okay again.

You got two ears and one mouth. You've heard everything, and so now you are an instant teacher of what I teach. That's what I am doing on these CDs and books, making instant teachers out there, whoever gets 'em, that they can use the same because Grandma said. It is meant to be left behind for people and children. They're going to be the caretakers. I always say that it is not us adults that own the world, it's the children, and we have got to take care of it for them. That's our job as adults.

Life has been a bumpy road. Like I tell people and elders, "Quit snottin' around and whinin'. It's a bumpy road. So stiffen up your backbone. You can do it. Don't be snottin', whinin' around about this or about that." I had all those people in Montezuma Wells coming up to me and saying, "We remember, Grandma. We won't be snottin' and whinin' around." It was funny, but it is true, you know. Getting older isn't easy, but this thing can tell you that you want to keep going, that you want to get up in the morning, that you got things to do. You got to keep goin'.

I don't want anybody helping me unless I absolutely have to have it. Like when I had both knees done, my granddaughter came, Nadine's daughter. Here I am right out of recovery on my walker, walking down the hall. She was flabbergasted. So were the nurses. They said nobody usually does that. But I wanted to try that knee out; I had that one done first, then this one. Again, I am on my walker going down the hall right out of recovery room. I had my hips done—same thing. They were there, some of them. My daughter was there. And I am on my walker out there walkin'. I was testing out, do I hurt? Does it pain me? Is it okay? If not, I want the doctor to know immediately that something was hurting. So I had to try it out. So only me, I could do it. So, I am on the walker with all of it. Same way with my foot when my doctor in Ashland—when I broke my foot in the Dharamsala over there and I had to walk on it. I damaged it, so then he put me out. It's a good thing, too, because he said it sounded like a carpenter. He said he had to take out a lot of bone and put that steel under my foot from my heel clear up to my toes, and two rods on both sides of my ankle—three bands and six screws in that ankle. Do I sit and snot around about it? No. I am grateful that I can walk on it. I am grateful that there's doctors like that. Knee doctors, hip doctors—I got good doctors. If it wasn't for you, all of us would be in wheelchairs. I am grateful to my doctor. Just give thanks. I give thanks. I always thank my doctors for all that they've done to keep me goin'. I have an electric wheelchair, too, and I have a carrier on the back, and I have portable wheelchairs, walkers, because sometimes it gets where I have to use them, you know. But I don't bitch and complain about it. It is a temporary thing, I say. It's just temporary. It's there for me.

I live and do everything, and I don't even get $900 a month in Social Security. But I don't fuss about it because the Creator—every first of the month, I say, "Thank you, Grandfather, for stretching my money." And it always works. Always. My daughter can tell you, I am not fussin' around about money. If she needs something or wants something, or a dress or something, it is always there for her. I pay all the bills and I run the household. But the Creator has always been so generous and so good to me throughout all these years.

I am a "notch victim." If I was born in 1926, I wouldn't be a notch victim, because I worked. I should be getting over a thousand dollars a month. But I am a notch victim, and I send monies to that all the time. I probably won't ever get it before I leave this world, but I still send monies to it. The senators and all will support and get that straightened out. They didn't put the age back there then when they started Social Security.

I worked hard raising my kids. You know, like I always say, when you pray, pray for your needs, not your wants. All of it has to do with life and living. It has nothing to do with church or religion. It is an opportunity and part of the way that we have been given, that opportunity to sit and talk to the Creator. People say it isn't tangible. Who cares? As long as the Creator is listening and something changes—I can't change it, but the Creator can. I know my limits, but I can put that option out there for you.

12

DRUGS AND ALCOHOL

I am so proud to be able to leave my words, which I speak as truth for our beloved earth and all the living things. Believe my words that all those little ones will one day be able to hear and follow, which I pray they do. How important it is to walk your path on this earth, as young as you are, with no cigarettes, no alcohol, no pills. Just think, someday, when you grow up and you get married and you're a dad, or you're a mother, and you are chemically free, just think of the legacy you have for your kids. You could say, "I haven't used any of this, so you kids don't need to use any of it, either." What an impact you are goin' to have on their life because you are walking it in such a great way now.

A long time ago I was a bouncer in Crescent City. They had me come down because the owner said I had that kind of disposition that I could talk to anybody. So, I became a bouncer. I was down there one night, and who came in but my husband and my youngest son. They were the first ones that I got by the scruff of the neck and threw out. They tried to come back in, and I duked it out with them, and they didn't get to come back in. After they sobered up they said, "Why did you do that, Mom?" I said, "I am not going to have some drunken idiots come around when I am the bouncer and act like you two did." I said, "You remember that. If you are drinkin' to drug your mind up to where you think you can do anything, don't do it around me or you'll get it." They looked at each other. I said, "It's your decision. I will do it again, and I will do worse next time." They were just astounded. "I am your husband!" "I don't care if you're the President. You gonna act like that, I'll just thump you up." I told my son, "I taught you better than that. You gonna follow this guy around, you know you're going to get the same thing he gets." He used to drink back then.

When I was gone he'd run down and get a tab going at the bar. I went down to the bar one time and come back and said to the bartender, "You know, I am not payin' any more bar bills. You're going to get that guy in here to work 'em off, because I am not paying them no more. You make a decision about that. That's between you and him. But I am not paying, and I am not giving you another dime for these tabs." Then my husband came home and I told him what I'd done. I called my brother clear up out of Pacifica, Washington. I told my brother to come and get him. He was a great big guy, my brother was, huge. My husband didn't even come up to his armpit. "You come down here and get this brother-in-law. Even if he's on a roof, you're going to take him, and I am going to pack his duds, and you take him up there with you. I am sick of it." So, he came down. I packed his oke gladstone—that's a cardboard box with his clothes in it. I gave it to my brother. I said, "He is down in Trinidad, California, and he is supposed to be roofing a house. I don't care if he is on the roof; you get him off of it and you take him up there with you. You tell him I said to find another Agnes to blame for his drinkin'." My husband told people I said this, I did that, and that's why he's drinkin'. And I told him never to come and knock on my door as long as he's like that.

He was up there in Washington with my brother for three and half months. I was in my office, and he gave me a call and said, "I am up here on Ninth Street. I just got back." I said, "What's the verdict? Did you find another Agnes up there to blame for your drinkin'? What are you going to do about it?" "I quit." "You sure?" I said, "Okay. You can come home, but I don't want that animal around me ever again. When you drink, you get to be an animal." He once even broke my big glass door because he couldn't get it open when I'd locked him out. That cost a bundle to put in that glass door. I said, "I don't want no more insanity around me ever again. You put that cork in the bottle, and you better keep it there because I am not going to put up with this insanity any more, ever." I said, "That's the rules."

For him, the way he was—he was a good guy, but that alcohol just made him into an animal, a man that I didn't want nothin' to do with. I said, "I don't want to try to sleep with one eye open all the time when you're gone, never knowin' when you're coming back or what kind of shape you're in and whether I am going to get shot, stabbed, or beat up." I said, "This insanity. I can't handle it anymore, being that I can't put the cork in the bottle for you or keep dumping them out. It's not my job. It's your job." And so what he said is he come home and that he quit.

One guy came and tried to get him to go drinkin' with him. I said, "If you go, you know the consequences." I said, "If you go out, I don't want you back. And I'll pack your clothes again. You make your own decision." He decided then that he didn't need any more alcohol. I said, "You've had enough now to float two ships. If you feel like you need any more, go away. I don't want you around me." When he came home, it seemed like—that's the good guy, that's the good guy that I saw in him when I first met him. The guy that respected his mother. He's all she had, and she was a medicine woman, but she was frightened for him. I said, "If you want your mother to live, then you straighten up your life."

It's a drug. People don't look at alcohol as a drug, but it is. It is a sedative. Why do you want to be in oblivion? What is there in your world that you want to cover up? What is inside of you that makes this choice? You don't like yourself somewhere that you need this as a crutch? Why do you want to make yourself a cripple? Because that's what it is, just a temporary crutch. Even if Dad used it, it's an unaccepted behavior. It is a drug. Why do you want to be drugged up? There's a choice here. What is the outcome of a choice that says, "I don't need it" or "I'll take it.

I'll drink it"? What is the outcome when you do that? What have you done to yourself to make that choice and say, "I'll drink with you"? What is going around in your head that you need to pity yourself? You need to cover up something? Or you think this will help you like yourself?

What is the excuse—because it is an excuse—of why you want to use a drug in the first place? Whether it is a pill, or whether it is alcohol, why do you feel so inadequate that you have to prop yourself up with that? It's crazy how people run that head. Then, the more you consume, who are you helping? Not yourself. You are killing yourself, but you are putting a roof over somebody else's head. It's making the cigarette people richer and richer. Alcohol people get richer and richer. The drug people get richer and richer. And where is your money? Leave it in your billfold, that's what. You're making somebody else dollars upon dollars upon dollars richer. Who is that somebody else? It is the people that's sellin' you the alcohol. You don't even know them, but you're helping them to get richer and richer and richer by you buying and consuming alcohol. It is the same with drugs. Who are you helping? Where is that money going that you're killing yourself the more you use it? But the money is going to someone else, and you don't even know that somebody else. It is sick, but it is a choice you are makin' for yourself.

Another thing—the money that you get, can you afford it? Are you into your allowance, your monthly allowance? Where else is that money supposed to be going? Are you stealin' from your own pocketbook? If you got a family, you're stealin' from family. If you have a wife, you are stealing from your wife. It's called thievery. How do you feel comfortable with that? I don't know how you can feel comfortable with that. To me, that's open-eyes thievery. You know what you're doing, but you don't think of the consequences or the costs. Besides, don't you want to live a long time? Alcohol is filtered through the liver. Pretty soon it's going to get your liver, then what are you going to do? Your liver could stop, and you slowly start getting yellow all over. You want to look like that? I have seen people who look like that because their liver shut down. Why don't you want to live a long time? What's wrong with you? What kind of thinkin' is that?

Creator gave you this life. You think you have a right to shorten it? Why are your choices going to this drug? Because it is not going to help you one bit. Same thing with cigarettes. Eventually you keep smoking and keep smoking, you are going to get cancer of the lungs. And it is not reversible. Why do you want to shorten your life? Because that is going to shorten it, too. Many people right here in my county are getting in jail, causing problems, because they're not running their head right. They're in jail, locked up like an animal because they're acting like one. If you don't want to be in a jail or something, you know, don't be putting anything down your mouth that the Creator didn't put in us. Alcohol, drugs, and cigarettes are all bad things. It's going to shorten your life if you use any of it. Nicotine and the carcinogens that they got in the cigarettes are god-awful. They even got formaldehyde in there, so think about it. They preserve organs from our body in formaldehyde.

Any of these drugs—I don't care what they got out there, it's going to affect your liver because it is the biggest filter in your body. It is slowly going to kill it off. It is true what I say. And it is sad, because your own two hands are pouring that down your own throat to slowly kill yourself. I've talked to universities all over this land, to young students about alcohol, about drugs. Why do you want to mess up your body and weaken it and weaken your thinkin' thing with any of these mind-altering drugs? Why? You're not good enough on your own? You can't run your life without this? Why are you weak? Because those things are literally like a crutch under you. Why you want to be crippled is beyond me. It tells me that you're not running your brain right and you're not as smart as I am, I guess, 'cause I smartened up way back there, and I am so glad I did or I wouldn't be sittin' here today.

My money goes for my upkeep and my daughter's upkeep and my house, not alcohol, pills, or drugs. No way. No way. That doesn't have a place in my vocabulary or my life. It is a choice that everybody has, to use and abuse. That's what you're doing, abusing yourself when you choose any of that stuff. If the Creator that brought us into this world wanted us to have it innocently, He would have created it innocently. Because it is all a mind-altering drug. You're so weak that you think that you need that stuff to run your brain? To me, that is really weakness. I don't care how big your size is, you're weakening your whole system.

You know, I teach this to my grandchildren and my great-grandson, who just turned seventeen. I told my grandson, "I sure love you, Grandson"—he's my great-grandson—"because I hear from my tribal people, even from tribal council members that are sitting on the tribal council, how good you are as a young man. They're so proud of you, how willing you are to jump in and help. They speak about you so well, that you don't use cigarettes and alcohol and drugs, and you're seventeen years old." Great big guy, over six foot, 215 pounds. Big kid. "But do you know what I think, Grandson? Someday you're going to be a dad, and just think the leverage you are going to use on those kids. You could tell your kids, 'I never used any of that stuff, never did smoke. I never used alcohol. I never used drugs, and you kids, I don't want you using it, either.' Just think of the legacy you could leave your children." I just told him that the other day.

I pray to God that kids continue to say no, no matter what Mom and Dad are doing. They don't have to do what Mom and Dad are doin', or Aunt or Uncle or anything. They already know that Mom and Dad aren't doing right, and they don't want it because they are smart enough to know what the outcome of it is. I was a First Indian Coordinator in Northern California for years. I dealt with alcohol and drugs where kids were coming to school hungry 'cause Mom and Dad drank up the money and the kids didn't have enough to eat before coming to school. I told the school system, "How can you teach a child sitting in a class-room that is all hungry, and here he is not paying attention to the teacher? What can we get these kids, some snacks or something?"

Then they began to have snacks at school for kids. Then a young boy was sent up to the teachers' room because he didn't have shoelaces. He couldn't understand—why am I getting punished? It was winter and the ground was wet, and they didn't want him falling out of his shoes and getting his socks wet and then sitting in school all day with wet feet and then gettin' sick. So, I had to go to the parents and tell them to get him some shoestrings. If they didn't, I would. If a kid came to school and didn't have a coat, he wasn't allowed out to play at recess 'cause it's chilly. I gathered up jackets from everybody I could get jackets from.

All these things I went through with children with alcohol and drugs. Getting to the parents, letting them know: you're teaching your kid. Do you want your kid to sit here and drink? How do you know he is not getting some of your stash? You are going to be all soused up all the time. Mom and Dad partying the night before, and here is a little kid still in diapers going around finding this bottle on the table. He gets a taste of it. As he grows, this party stuff continues. He get more tastes of it. So when he gets bigger, in his teens, he wants that taste. It's terrible what parents do with their kids, even when they're little. They want that taste. Why are you teaching this kid that it is okay for him to get to drinkin', too? You want him drinkin'? It's sad how you're doing this. I started the first Alcoholic Anonymous meetings over there. They never had one. But I made a decision: put the cork in the bottle. We'd gather up. We had songs. Those that could sing and straighten up and had a drum, bring your drum. Sing us a song. You can do things without a prop; you could do a lot of stuff. Those that got jobs, I would go up to the Bureau of Indian Affairs and say, "I need some startup money for clothes for so-and-so and so-and-so, so that they can go to work in the fish plant. They need rain boots. They need aprons. They need rain clothes. They need gloves. I need some startup money for them." So, we got lots of people changing. They have a leak in their roof, they need some money to fix their roof. I got a lot of people going to Alcoholics Anonymous, and it really worked for lots and lots of people.

When you're using alcohol, you know, cirrhosis of the liver—
you ever see anybody's liver that has cirrhosis in it? It is horrible.
I've seen pictures of where they cut parts of it off and people are
still living. Here you are, and you're gettin' cirrhosis of the liver,
and you're having lung problems, and you're still using alcohol
and drugs. It's insane, absolutely insane. You're making a bloom-
ing idiot out of yourself when you get so drunked up you're not
hearing nothing from anybody. You're off in some kind of la la
land or something. Alcohol is just a crutch.

If you're smoking, you know eventually you are going to get
emphysema, and emphysema and lung cancer are not reversible.
Think about it, if you smoke. When you are buying cigarettes,
you are putting a shingle on somebody else's roof and it's shortening your life, and you're going to get lung cancer sure as God
made green apples. You know you're going to get lung cancer.
I have seen people with lung cancer; it is a devastating thing.
I've taken care of some of these people that didn't stop the cigarettes soon enough. It's hard to be around somebody breathing
that stuff, because when they are on that oxygen, I catch myself
breathing like that. It makes me feel like I got to take a deep
breath. It's god-awful to see somebody that's like that, and it's
a horrible thing. Pretty soon they get so gaunt—you know, all
sunken in in their chest. It is so sad. And to be hooked up to
oxygen because you smoked and got your lungs in such a terrible
shape that you're barely alive. And it's not right.

Do you want your kids to be that way? You better quit smokin'
in front of them. Even second-hand smoke is bad for kids. I pray
that when you get to using nicotine that you think of all these
things. There are more carcinogens in cigarettes than there was in
1972 when I smoked. But I gave it up because I didn't want lung
cancer. I didn't want that to happen to me. So if you don't want
lung cancer, then you better throw away those nails in your coffin.
That's what I call those cigarettes. It's shortening your life, that's
for sure. Some people never learn. They still smoke the cigarette.
Cigarettes got it that way, that nicotine and those carcinogens. I

had a daughter-in-law that smoked and had emphysema and was still buying cigarettes. That's kind of an insanity.

I am glad I sit here today talkin' about this stuff. I have a son that's seventy and my baby is sixty-three, they are all alcohol-free. I am so happy about that. It's a choice they made. It's not that I went and stopped them doin' it. Rationality. They rationalized that they didn't need it. So they don't use it, and I am so proud of them. I done my job. I pray that you, too, can do that. Nobody can put the cork in the bottle if you're drinkin'. Nobody can put that cork in the bottle but yourself. If you want your money to go down the rat hole, keep spending it on alcohol and drugs and cigarettes. You're getting poorer and poorer and slowly killing yourself, shortening your life, and I don't know for the life of me how anybody with a brain, half a brain even, don't want to live long. And you're killing yourself slowly, inches by inches, and it's sad because I don't think you got a right to do that. The Creator gave you this life, and look how you're destroying yourself.

I pray that when you read this that whatever you're using, you could stop, because it is only a crutch. Why be a cripple when you don't have to? It's a choice you make, but you can make a choice to let it all go. I pray that you do, for a healthier body and healthier mind and a healthier life. And if you have children, just think how you are salvaging theirs because you can say, "I quit. I don't use it anymore, and I don't want to use it because . . . " and tell them why. Explain it. Explain that you want them to live a long time, so give them that, that beautiful walk in front of them as your job, leading your children to not be putting things into their body or smoking around them, because even second-hand smoke is horrible for children. Even if you're smoking outside, you are showing them that it is okay behavior, and I don't think it is good, any of it.

I don't want you to forget that you always have a choice, no matter what your age is. Think of these things. You have a choice, so make a good one. Someday you're going to grow up and maybe be a parent of a teenager. What kind of parent do you want to be to your children? One that's chemically free so that you can tell your kids that alcohol, drugs, and tobacco is not an accepted behavior? Wouldn't you want to tell your kids that? I pray you would. I pray that you will learn to teach them that way, to stay away from these things because it wasn't meant to be. But you have that choice

Please make a good decision with your life. All you have to do, from sun up to sun down, is say, "No, I don't need it." You can convince yourself to say that. Just one day at a time. That's what all life anywhere can do, one day at a time. You can do it. Be big about it. Be grateful. Be grateful just for life, that you can do this for yourself. Think logically. I pray that you can make a difference with your body by how you run your brain. You can do it, because your brain is strong enough that you can make all these decisions without any of those mind-altering drugs. It's easy. It's one step at a time. One day at a time. Can't you handle yourself one day to stay away from alcohol, drugs, or pills, or anything? One day. Can you run this thing good enough to stop one day? If you can stop from morning to night, as your head lays down on the pillow, what an accomplishment. One day. The next day you get up and think of the same thing again. You got a handle on it. When you get up, just remember, "I don't need it today." Pretty soon you'll think, "Gosh, I've got a week in, I've got a month in, I've got a year in, I've got two years in," and you did it.

The pats on your back, you earned them. I say that's the strength of this thinkin' thing. How you run it. You ask yourself, do I really need it? Can I afford it? Can I shorten my life, or can I live a long time? Can I just pocket the money or put it in the bank or help my family instead of squandering it? Because that's what you're doing when you're buying alcohol, drugs, or tobacco—you're squandering it. I am so proud that I quit that.

I call it a sign of weakness when you bend down and start smokin, and you bend down and you start takin' alcohol, and you bend down and start takin' drugs. All a sign of weakness in you. Why do you want to be weak? Why do you need these as a crutch to prop you up? You can make all these decisions without mind-altering drugs. And I pray that someday, if I am still on this planet, you will come to me and say, "I did it, Grandma. I made a good choice." I pray that I will hear some of these voices and see some of you that have made that choice. Don't go down that awful, awful road. Stay on the Red Road. Come along with me.

13
GIVING THANKS, LETTING GO

When you leave all of these chemicals and elements that kept you chained and you let it go, you are giving thanks to the Creator. If you listen good, the Creator will give you guidance, and it's not the doorknob above your head. It's the beloved Creator.

I always say I am nothing without my Creator. And I am not talkin' church or Christianity. I am talking about the freedom of each and every one of us to reach out to our Creator. There is only one beloved Creator, but there's many paths. I don't care what path you choose, but if you can walk your talk—meaning that you can walk in truth, where you don't lie to yourself—then you're not lying to your children or the neighbors or to anybody you run into every day. You are walking truth as I walk truth.

Maybe truth to me is not what truth is to you, but that's okay. I think that once you start being truthful to yourself, you'll get ahold of it as to what it means to you. So, when you do make that choice, lift your head high, because the Creator is in your life, our Maker, the one that created all of us from the get-go. Adam and Eve didn't have belly buttons, but we do. Especially mothers and women. We are the givers of life. I am so thankful that the Creator has been in my life for many, many years.

As I said before, I didn't want to walk the spiritual path, but it kept coming and kept coming. I didn't think I was worthy. So what I did was, when I did this spiritual path, I created a

basket beside me and put my other self in it with all the characteristics, the bad ones or whatever, and forgave her. Shut the lid
and forgave her. She's still there today, and I give thanks to her
because she stood this one up, so I forgive that other me in all its
entirety. I feel good telling you today after all these many, many
years of keeping her in there. I feel good that this one stood up
and walked with the beloved Creator, which is an opportunity
anybody could have. Again, it doesn't make you have to get down
on your bended knee. You can pray to the Creator when you're in
a canoe or sittin' by the river or in the shower or on the john—
wherever—giving thanks just for being and taking up this little
spot on the Earth Mother's face. Learn to be grateful and to give
thanks to the beloved Creator. It took the Creator to make all of us.

We are all from the same God. We're all connected. I don't care
what the color of your skin is. I love you because you have being
and you have creation from the same Creator that created me.
He just made us into a different flower garden. Now we went and
we made another flower garden. We have done that. We all made
different colors. It's our right. If I took the skin off of every one
of us, we'd all look alike. So, we are connected.

Learn to stop the bias and prejudice. Stop being judgmental
about yourself and the neighbors. There's only one judge, and
that's our beloved Creator. Walk your talk. Speak truth. Be kind
to yourself. Learn to teach your kids kindness and respect and
love, that life is sacred. It was given to us, so do the best you can
by giving thanks every morning when you get up, and bless it to
wake up. I about died how many times in my life already, but I
give thanks again that I can wake up and have one more day. I am
grateful for one more day because all life can do only one day at
a time. I pray that you have a privilege to change the way you're
doin'. If what you're doing is not meeting with some of the family
members, what you're putting down your throat, your lungs, or
whatever—change. Stop. You want to be loved, then act it.

Actions are greater than words. People watch. People know
whether you are walkin' your talk or not. I can walk down the

street and tell you who has got their life going good and who doesn't. You could do that, too. If I can do it, you can do it. Don't be using excuses: "I can't because . . . I can't because . . . " Quit snottin' and whinin'. Life is a bumpy road. I am going to be ninety-one pretty soon, and it's a bumpy road, so don't think that snottin' and whinin' around is going to do you any good. Take good care of yourself. It is a great gift the Creator gave you, so take care of your body and your life. Run it in a good way, a healthy way. Eat right. Many of us are getting so big, it's sad. I was an *oh-my-gosh* size, too, and I had high blood pressure, so I took control of myself and said, "I am going to eat better," and I did. And when I got 180-something pounds off, my high blood pressure disappeared. I was crying, I was so thankful to me. Nobody did this but me. I am so thankful that I took charge of my body and got my weight down, and I still want to lose some more. So, I eat good. I eat a lot of fruit and a lot of vegetables. I treat my body with thankfulness. I am glad I got life. I have the right to be able to treat my body in a good way. I hope that you think about life and how grateful you are to have it.

If you're not eating right and you are putting on too much weight, use that brain to change. Nobody can change you but yourself. If you want to live, then you change. I pray that something I have said has made you turn your life around and get a good foot forward. Give yourself a pat on the back because you made a change, because you tell the truth to nobody but yourself. Bless you. Thank you ever so much.

14

BULLYING

That bullying thing. You know, I have talked to all my children and little ones growing up about bullying. I believe it gets started through the parents and how the parents treat their kids. If you're going to bring a child into the world, they got to be wanted. They got to be loved. If you care about your child, you'll love it. When you love your child, you won't be hitting on them. Many parents slap their kids around and scream and holler and voice-control, you know—then they know when their parents' voices gets this certain pitch, they're supposed to do whatever they are tellin' them. That's sad, too. If they whip on their kids, that is not right, either.

I worked in Northern California in an Indian sector as a coordinator between the school and the home. This one young Indian kid would get on the bus, and he'd be frightening with all the other little kids. I checked it out and found out his mother whipped on him all the time, and now he was going to get kicked off the bus. I went to the mother and said, "You want to drive your son back and forth to school every day?" "No," she said. "Well, I am going to tell you something. They're going to kick him off the bus because every time he gets on it, he gets to fightin' with some of the other kids. So I am going to ask you to do something. If you don't want to bus your child to and from school, then you stop hitting on him, because he thinks that's an accepted behavior. That's why he's beatin' on these other kids. Can you change?

Can you hug him and do some other form of—if he needs to be corrected—time out? Make him sit down instead of hitting on him, because he is hitting on somebody else and is going to get kicked off the bus. If you could try that, do that. Change, and apologize to him. He is big enough to know; he's in the third grade, and he knows right from wrong. And if you could explain and apologize about your behavior on him, and start hugging him and telling him you love him, that will change his behavior, and it will change him when he gets on the bus."

One of the young Indian kids hated white people. I said, "Well, okay. Come in my office and bring your gun with you. We'll go out in the street, and the first white person will be your mother. Shoot her." His eyes got big. I said "Your mother's a white woman, isn't she? She's my niece, isn't she? So stop thinkin' like that." I was a hard-nosed counselor. No snottin' around, you know. You snottin' around, don't get around me. I told them, "The Creator gave you a backbone. Use it. You want to be wishy-washy, that's only for jellyfish. You're going to have to start doing a better thing with your life. How you run this thing is how you're going to behave."

Mothers, if you're going to have a child, when that child gets two years old or three years old, how you treat it will mean how it will behave. If you love your child, let them know that. Hug them. Hold them. Don't scream at them. Don't be beatin' on them, because they're going to find somebody else to be beatin' on. Because of your behavior, they think that's an accepted way to be treated. It causes them to be a bully. They're going to go to the school grounds, and they're going to find somebody they can thump on. It's going to cause that child problems. It's all wrong, that type of behavior. I hope that mothers would, when you borne your child, love it. Give it that beginning hug and that reassurance when they get to walking and listening and hearing your voice.

It is a simple thing to hold your child and say, "I love you." My kids are all grandparents. A couple of them are great-grand-parents, and to this day they call me and are always saying, "I love you, Mother." Now, why would they do that at that age? It's because I taught them when they were little. They still tell me that, even though they got grandchildren. Even when they call me, come see me, they always say, "I love you, Mother." It is so precious to my heart that I have done my job in a good way.

My sons didn't bully anybody around. They didn't go beating on other kids. I am proud of that. The history that they have is part of my leadership, I believe. It is because I love them to this day. I've always loved my children, and I felt so grateful that the Creator gave them to me. I watched after them, whether they were warm, whether they were hungry, whether they needed a drink of water. And that's another thing: I never let them drink a whole bunch of pop, even growing up. So don't be giving your kids a lot of pop. It is going to make them get fatter and fatter and fatter, and it's not good for you. They'd be much healthier—all of you would.

Learn to be grateful and to be thankful, and teach that to your children along with stopping the bullying. Teach a child kindness. If a child can understand kindness and he can grasp ahold of what kindness means, you know, if you have kindness in you, you'll always be treated kindly. I taught my children that all of the things like that—smiles and happiness, joy, compassion and love, laughter, and all of these things—were their inside job. I couldn't give it to them; they had to create it. So, your children have to create it. You can't give it to them, either, but you can teach them about it, how they can grasp these things and understand even when they're little.

Teach them that you love them. Show them that you love them. Your behavior is louder than words. Learn to love your kids so that when they get to school age, they learn to get along, and it'll be easier for them. They won't be having a hard time. A lot of times when you treat your child like beatin's okay and he goes out and finds somebody else to beat on, you're going to cause him or her to get in trouble. So love your child, because when he gets like that and then his grades go down and he is failing in school, then he gets sent to the teacher or the principal's office. Then the teachers are on him, then he goes home with this report card and his parents or caregivers are on him, and he feels kind of boxed in. So, many of them, what do they do? They go kill themselves. This is frightening. I don't believe that anybody has a right to take their life, because that was the greatest gift that our Creator gave us, was life.

I hope that when you read this and you are going to have a child, please love it. And when it gets here, help it to have all of these good things. Talk to him about all the good things that they need to have inside, because when you teach that to your children, then others will treat them with kindness and love and respect. It is a great thing for you to have respect for yourself. Then you don't get in trouble anywhere you go throughout your life. If you have respect for yourself, then you have complete control of your behavior and you're doing good with it. You're walking your talk, as I say. This means truth to yourself. When you have truth inside of you, then everything that you say is truth to anybody else. I always say that I can only teach how people should answer and be truthful.

When I walk and do things in front of my beloved Creator, it's through that personal integrity. Honesty is a great gift that I have in me that was taught by my mother and my dad. My dad told us girls, "When you grow up and you get married and your husband beats on you, it is his fault. If he does it again, it is yours." You have to be able to handle that and be able to let people know that you're not going to be beat on. My dad says, "You girls are not a punching bag for no man." We were taught that.

I don't put up with a mother screamin' at her kids, either. If I hear about it, I try to go over and talk to them. If there's alcohol and drugs, I try to deal with that. So, that's a no-no, too. Your children watch your behavior whether you realize it or not. And they can be healthy if you treat them with love, honor, and respect. I pray that you do so that when they go to school, they then have these qualities and they are treated good in school.

I think that if you can teach your child to sing, or if you have a musical instrument—when you create those types of qualities, the kids can kind of fit and belong. Our Native people have an especially hard time because they haven't been taught by their peers how to fit and belong. This is why my dad made us all learn music. It was a good thing for me to feel like I fit and belonged in a public school, because I played the piano, the violin, the banjo, and the guitar. And like I said before, I didn't go to the Indian school like my brothers and sisters did.

All of these things that I'm talkin' to you about, it's a good thing that I listened to my parents. I am glad that they loved me and hugged me and covered me when I was little, that they come in and tell me goodnight and that you love me. To this day my middle daughter that takes care for me and lives with me, she never goes to bed without saying, "Good night, Mother. I love you." And it is so precious to my heart to hear that. And she is a great-grandmother. So, I feel like I have done my job when I have taught my children what it means to have respect for yourself and to honor yourself and have these good qualities. My kids are grown. If you ever want to go and ask them did I teach them these things, they'll tell you, as old as they are, that yes, I did. They had to make all these things happen inside of themselves. I couldn't give it to them.

They weren't lazy kids, either. They had their chores, and they did them. When they were nine years old I told them I was not their maid no more, that they had to learn to sort their clothes and put it in the washing machine. My boys had to learn to iron their clothes. I said, "Someday you kids are going to have children, and so what I am teaching you, you are going to teach your children." I told my sons, "You're going to learn to cook, you're going to learn to wash; you're going to learn to iron your clothes. If you have to sew a button on, you can do it. Someday you are goin' to get married, and maybe your wife will get sick or something and you have to do her work. So, you got to learn these things." My son is a great-great-grandfather, and he can tell you that he is still a wonderful cook. He can still wash his clothes, he can still iron. Whatever it is, he's still been able to do that. All my boys, they learned to cook. They were really good cooks. I would go and visit my sons, and my youngest son, he'd jump up the next morning, and he never told him he'd be out there makin' breakfast for me. It was so precious, so special those times.

I taught my sons not to be hitting on their sister, either, because she is not a punching bag for you boys. I stopped that type of behavior immediately with my children. They grew up that way, too; they weren't going around punching on somebody unless somebody tried to beat them up; then they had to defend themselves.

How you treat your child with love is one of the greatest gifts that they will pick up. Every child needs love, and that's why you bring them into the world. I pray that I have said something today that will help your kid not to get in trouble on the school grounds, not to be a bully, not to be shoving people around or using swear words. That's not a good thing to be doing. I pray that you can say some good things and hug your child day or night or whenever you get the opportunity, to reassure them that you care, that you watch, and that you know how they are. So, all that I am teaching you, if you can teach that to your child, you will have less problems as that child grows up. I appreciate it, if you could do that.

Don't forget, hug your child as much as you can, and that means Dad, too. Dad, you tell the children that you love them and that you care about them. My dad did that to me. He loved us kids. I pray that you can do that. Reassure them. If they get into trouble, sit down and talk to them about the behavior. You're the teacher at home, and the teacher is the parent at school. So, let the kids know that the teacher is going to be watching out and see if you are behaving at school, too. You won't get into any trouble if you listen to these things and do what I tell you. So I want to thank you for listening. Thank you so much.

15

TEEN SUICIDE

I work hard around the country to try to salvage our young kids. Some kids that are really young are committing suicide because they get a failing grade in school or the teachers put 'em up in the principal's office to be punished because they're not keepin' up. The school is on 'em, then they go home and Mom and Dad are on 'em, so they feel like they're boxed in, and what do they do? They can't handle it, so they kill themselves. It is sad that they get to that point in their life where they feel like they can't go forward.

I have wished that I could hold 'em and talk to them about how precious life is, to not throw it away, that they have been taught by someone that they are no good or they're not worthy, or they're dumb or they're scatterbrained. These derogatory terms are used by both parents sometimes, so the child feels like, "I am nothing, I am no good." When he gets that in his head, he doesn't care about anything—life, whether he lives or not. He doesn't seem to care about an education. He doesn't want to listen to anybody, and he's kind of boxed himself in to the point where he can't see the sunshine, as I say.

It hurts my heart that they become so fragile in their feelings. Just like a piece of glass, they crack and they break because they can't see a tomorrow, or a tomorrow or a tomorrow, feel that they're not worthy, they're no good. Life is the most precious gift we have, so join me, too, and help salvage these children. Help to mentor or to say good things to them. Help them in any way you can, any kids that you know of that are around you and that this is happening to. Also, wherever you live, if they have a juvenile hall, check out those kids and see if they're being molested, see if they're being treated right. It's a good thing for any citizen to kind of look around and see if this is happening. Watch after the young people. Like I said, you don't have to have borne a child to love it, you just need to care about 'em. When I was the First Coordinator in Del Norte County and in Crescent City, if children didn't have warm jackets in the winter, I would go around to second-hand stores and gather up a bunch of jackets and give 'em to these kids. I didn't have to do that.

Kids were coming to school, and there was no milk for their cereal at home because their parents drank. They come to school maybe just having a piece of toast, and their tummies are growling. So, I got them to bring in snacks in the schoolroom for kids, because no child is going to be listening to a teacher if his tummy is growling. I told that to the district years ago. Then I would go out to the parents and see what's happening. And if it's alcohol and drugs, I would lay it on 'em. "I got your kids some jackets because you're using the money and you're not even paying attention that he was cold." I have done a lot of stuff like that. I don't begrudge one moment of all I done for kids, all kids.

I used to go out and gather money to take the kids down to the YMCA. We lived where it is surrounded by water everywhere, and I told the kids, "You got to learn to swim." So I would go out, get them tickets to go down to the Y, and have the lifeguards down there sitting up watching and helping these kids to learn to swim. "Someday," I said, "learning to swim may save your life or somebody else's." I said, "There's water everywhere, and you need to learn to swim." Even then, at those times, I said the water inside us, the water outside of us, you know, is a healing thing. I said, "This is good for you." They lay out there, and I taught 'em how to float, and they blessed the water and lay on top. How beautiful that feeling is to experience. I did things like that, helping kids.

I been like that, always helping kids, bringing kids home, kids crying because Dad did this and Mom did that. If I had room, I would take 'em. If not, I would sit and hold and talk to them, all of them, just to get things straightened out. I have helped a lot of lives in a lot of good ways, and I am proud of that because I care about life. I don't care whose life.

I had to work, and I was an employed one parent. I was one parent to those kids, and I said, "You got to help." They had to start learning to wash their clothes, pick up after themselves, lay out their school clothes for the next day, all of that. I said, "I got to be out there workin'. You kids got to help." And that's the way to do it. It's our job as elders in a community to watch after our children. I do that. I am always inquisitive and want to know, and for sure, my god, it hurts my heart to go through these kinds of things.

I am working with people up in Eugene who are wanting the state or somebody to help get us some grant money to build a transition house for these young people. I been workin' with them, I've talked to the tribal peoples. Let's salvage our children together. Let's build a place for them where they can have three squares a day, where they can shower, where they can have a bed, where they can help one another and be taught by First Nation teachers. We'll watch over them. Us elders will have a panel of elders to see that it functions in that way. There's not a transition house for our young people; they get in reformatories or they get into prison. I've worked in the prison system many, many times over the years trying to salvage a young person. Some of them are still alive to this day and are parents now. So we want to build a place, a transition house, to stop the recidivism of them going out on the street and trying to live and stealing, and getting caught and being put back inside the walls again.

I been workin' hard on these kinds of things for our young people, and I hope that anybody that can help can work and do something for our youth. Just because you didn't borne that child doesn't stop your obligation. We got to care about our young kids, and I would like to see a transition place. I would like the people up there in Eugene to be able to accomplish that. One man has fifty acres that already has got a building on it. If we can get a grant, we can build the beds and a kitchen and everything that goes in it for our young people.

I have taught them behind the walls to help kids to bead. I said, "If you can learn to bead, you'll never be broke, because people will always buy beadwork. You can always sell it." There are a lot of these young guys doing beadwork. I worked with a lady that is a dear friend of mine. We got beads and needles and leather inside the walls and were teaching young men to bead. Some of them didn't want to, but there was a road for them. We had the patterns all mapped out and fixed on cloth and stuff, and all they had to do was follow the markings on it to make a rose with the colors and beads and everything. One of the young men said, "That's women's work," and he didn't want to do the rose. Well, he ended up being top beader. I taught the kids, "If you can learn to bead, you'll never be broke." So, that one young person thinks that he is failing, and he can't see the sunshine. But we could find him, and we could put him in this place and help him to stand and to be accounted for so that he can someday say, "I made it." And this is a place that everybody should want to help in, this transition house.

I would like to talk to our lady governor, Kate Brown, to see if there's any funds anywhere to help put a transition house up for our young people that get into trouble, to know that somebody cares for them. This is why everybody got erasers on the pencil, because everybody makes a mistake somewhere along. We're not all perfect. So we can have this transition house for these young people so they can have three squares a day, and they can have a change of clothes and a place to lay their head. I pray that this happens so that they won't have to go out and rob and steal, get caught, and go back in again because their parents have moved away and they washed their hands of them. I think that's sad. I would like to help them in that way somehow.

The greatest gift the Beloved gave us was life, and after that he gave us this thinkin' thing called the brain. So they could get a handle on runnin' their brain—nobody's runnin' their brain but them—they could run their brain and say, "I can do it." If you think that you can't do it, then you won't. But if you can, you will. So stop the negative conversations to yourself that you can't. Just like the little train, you know, the little choo choo—*you can, you can, you can*. If you could put that one thing into your head—that you can accomplish something—then just start with one thing, whatever it is, one thought that is a positive thought, that you can do something.

There's things that you can do if you get caught up in juvenile hall; you're still a life. It is our obligation to see that you get opportunities to be able to work your way back out of there. Your head got you in there, and your head can get you out. Think about it. If you run your head right, you can get out of there. If you got in there, it was your head got you in there. Your brain, the way you did something—you made a mistake. That's all you did. Think of it as a mistake. You can correct it. Nobody but you can correct it. You have that opportunity, the way you run your brain. As I say, that's the longest journey you'll ever make, from your brain to your heart.

Think positive. Nobody, I believe, has a right to take their life because, to me, you're precious. As long as you're breathing, you're precious. No matter what you've done, there's always a way to get out of mistakes. There is a way. There is sunshine if you run your head right. The longest walk and the hardest walk any of you will ever have to do is from your thinkin' thing—the brain— eighteen inches to your heart. My daughter Nadine says, "Why eighteen inches, Mom? It's shorter than that." I said, "I know, but eighteen inches is an odd number, and when people hear eighteen, they say, 'Oh, Grandma said eighteen inches to your heart.'" And when you get to your heart, you know, I call that the "ah ha" stage. When you get there you know who you are, what you're to do, and where you're going. So I pray that you run your life from your thinkin' thing to your heart and do a good job. How you lead your life is how healthy you'll be. If you get depressed and you get down, it's your brain that got you there, and it's your brain that can get you out of there if you run it right.

So, if you get down and you lose the sunshine, your brain can bring you back up to the sunshine belt. Remember that. I am going on ninety-one, and I prayed to God that I could continue on at least another ten years because I feel like my little family still needs me as a guide and a person to strengthen and uphold and love. The greatest thing that you got is love. Love is all there is. If you want love, you got to have it in your own body. And I am not talking about eagle love. I am talking about the love and the joy of being just for being. Taking up this little spot on Earth Mother's face is a loving thing. It's a gracious thing. I pray that you save a life, even one. You can't put a price on one life. If even one can salvage that one, you know, it's worth it all.

16

A MESSAGE FOR MEN AND WOMEN

If you were world leaders right here today, you would be aware of many of the things I have written about already. I think that the greatest thing I could tell any leader is that the men have this feminine conscious inside of them, which should soften them down a lot. They got to realize that it took a woman's body to bring them into this world, which is a humbling thought. It is a humbling word for them to say, "Yes, I remember my mother, who gave me life." If they can admit that, then they are beginning to think in a good, balanced way about the feminine in their body. So, never forget that, fellows. If you're reading this, remember, there is that woman inside of you that you need to check out. Help her to manifest herself in your life by being kind, by having compassion for life, for your own life. And that means admission that your mom gave you life into this world. That admission should make you feel more humble and thankful and gracious about being in this world.

I know that our beloved Creator has both man and woman. It's a he/she God, and I always admire that thought. When I think about, it that it is in my life, I better be walkin' my talk. I better be speaking truth that the Creator said He created us all in likeness so that no matter who is listening to me has those aspects in their body, the feminine, the masculine. So, that's your job: each and every one of us is to balance that and to walk with that graciousness and humbleness that what I say is true. If you don't believe it, check me out. Go to a psychologist. Go to a place where you can read about the feminine inside of you, you guys. Check me out—girls, women—check me out. Am I speakin' the truth? You study up. When I went back to college at Southern Oregon University I studied psychology, and the first person I studied was myself.

I was so glad I took that subject because it sure opened my eyes about a lot of things. If you go to college, be sure and take that subject because it is a great healing thing. It's a subject that you need to understand. Everybody needs to understand, whether you go to college or not. There's psychology books in libraries all over this country. Study it. When you do, you study yourself. Learn to balance yourself. You'll be calmer. You'll be a nicer person, and all the good things will begin to flow out of your life. Can you do it? Would you do it? Will you do it? It's for your benefit that I am talking about anybody can go and do this. Any woman, any man, any young girl, any young boy can study this. And when you become balanced, you will fit better in your home; you'll fit better in your community or anywhere you go. You'll fit and belong because you have read and studied yourself and have that under-standing. I know that if the President was right here—for him to take the job that he has taken, or any of our presidents—they have that knowledge. They probably don't speak of it as I do, but they do have that knowledge because every one of them has gone to college. Every one of them knows law. So I know that they had to run over these words about the feminine inside of them.

My prayer is that I can pray—and you can join me—every-body, let us pray that the rulers in this world will begin to look within themselves and balance themselves. When they do that, they won't be so macho and want wars and killings. Would they mind if we got a gun and come over and shot their grandma and shot their grandparents, shot their kids, would they like that?

Well, that's what wars do. Teaches us to make murderers out of our children, and no mother likes that.

I have had relatives and brothers in the wars, and I was scared for them. I prayed for their safety, and they came home from the wars. My brother Terry came home in a medical ship because he contracted that malaria over there, but he come home from that. He was at the Battle of Malinta Hill when they raised the flag over there. I was so proud of my brothers that were in the wars, and my cousins and uncles. My uncles were in that Desert Storm down there, and they released them and let my uncles come home because they were over-age. I was so glad to run up and hug them and that they got out of there and got to come back.

We have in our family a lot of relatives that were in the wars in the past. Did you know that at all the wars that have been in effect in the United States, the biggest contingent in the wars was our First Nation people? It's a sad thing to say that, but it's also an honorable thing how every one of our tribal nations were told in the beginning to lay down your arms and never pick up your arms again. Yet, they drafted them and put them in a war. They weren't supposed to do that. Once they laid down their arms, they weren't supposed to do that. Yet it ended up that the First Nation people all over this United States were the biggest contingent in every war. Check it out. You can quote me. I have done my history.

We have one of the best and the most beautiful monuments out of Jefferson, Oregon. This monument is only for the First Nation veterans of the United States, and it is the only one in the United States and in the world. Two or three years ago I cut the ribbon. We got the names of all the code talkers that were instrumental in the wars, helping us to win the wars as we have because of the code talkers. We're all First Nation people. I have all of the names that are on that monument. I was crying. What an honor to see the names of our code talkers all in one place. So many of my relatives are on there. If you're a veteran and you want your name on there, get ahold of me. I can tell you who to call and the number to call. It only costs fifteen dollars to put your name on a plaque, to put it up there. If you're a First Nation person and your name hasn't been put on there, let me know and we'll see that it gets on there.

Think about these things that I have talked about today. It's things that maybe don't concern you, but it should concern you because I talked about it collectively and individually. Take what you need and walk with it, because it will help your life. Think about your walk. Are you doing it right? Your brain is supposed to be ruling your body, and when it does, when you walk, are you walking the good path? Are you on the good path? And if you're not, why are you resisting? Because you are not runnin' your head right if you're resisting. Please, use that thinkin' thing in a good way, for betterment of your life. It's a healthier way, and you will live longer. God bless. Thank you.

17

I AM BALANCED

I was told a long time ago that the Creator created us in His likeness. That means I am man/woman. I have this masculine consciousness in my body, the men have the woman's consciousness, and it needs to balance. The Creator said He made us just like Him, so the Creator is man/woman, Grandfather/Grandmother. I really realize that, so I am balanced.

It took a long time for me to realize that I had overdone it. I was more masculine than I was feminine. One time when I was young, maybe twenty, twenty-five, I looked in my closet and I saw an old woman's things, and I thought, my god, where's this woman? Are you in there? I began to look at my clothes, and I didn't have no high heels, no ruffles, no nylons, no gowns, no skirts. Just sweat pants, jeans, slacks, all this stuff. And I thought, I got to change. So, I began to dress different. I began to study and read about how that masculine part is in us and how it has to balance. I could see how the Creator had His hands in that, too. Then I began to realize, yes, I have to balance the masculine inside me and bring out the woman and the feminine part of who I am. But I always have to remember that masculine part, too, to simmer it down and don't be so bossy and screechin' and scrimmaging around like I used to be. I straightened up and I balanced myself. I believe this is why we have wars around the world, because the men that have the women's consciousness are not balanced with that. They have to be macho, so they create these wars because they want money, money, money, money. I always say, when is enough enough? Do we have to go around killin' everybody and teaching our kids to go to war? Raising them up to be killers and to get out there and to kill? It is not right. It is not right.

Yet, I honor the veterans that have gone on and gave their all and went up to the Star Nation with our beloved Creator. All of those that are alive, when I know they're veteran, I hugged them and shook their hand. "Thank you for the freedom that I have in this land." I am always gracious to our veterans and always there for them. If there is a need that I can help in any way with my two hands, I am there. I don't have to know who they are, just to know they're a veteran. If I can help in any way, I get in there and try to do what I can.

I don't believe that many of our veterans are being treated right. I know there's some out on the streets, homeless. It shouldn't be like that for our veterans. They laid their life on the line for our freedom, and we shouldn't be allowing them to be out there homeless. So if you know of a homeless veteran, do what you can to help that homeless veteran. We can do a lot of things, all of us, no matter what age, even if you're in a wheelchair. Sometimes I am in a wheelchair and I can still function. I can still do things. I pray that you do, too. Think about our freedom and how it came about for us. And about balance.

If you are a man reading this, balance the feminine inside of you; like when you buy a gift for your wife, that's the feminine in you matching the feminine in your wife. If you're giving flowers, that's what you're doin. The feminine is speaking out from inside your body. Same with women. If you are bossing around, screaming around, you know, that's that masculine part. Simmer down. Bring out the feminine, the gracefulness, the kindness, the love, the respect, and all that. We owe it to ourselves, ladies, to balance ourselves. I hope that the women that are reading this have checked themselves out and can do that. Thank you again. I appreciate it.

When us Grandmas came together in 2004 out of Phoenicia, New York, I prophesied then that more and more women were empowering themselves, standing up and taking prestigious jobs all over the world, and it's slowly happening. Who would have ever thought that we'd have a woman governor here in the state of Oregon? I am very proud. I met Kate Brown some time ago, and I am very proud that she's one of our givers of life. And I always say that us women have an invisible umbilical cord to the earth because we're natural nurtures. I think more and more women are going to be standing up and being professors at universities, and I think if woman were to rule this world, it would stop the wars, because no mother wants her kid to grow up to learn to kill.

We need peace; we need harmony; we need love through-out the world so that we can have peace all over the world. The Grandfathers, there's over 25,000 of them touring the globe. I have talked to them a couple times now, told them that I really like their walk. They're doing great, too. They're mentoring young men. I told those men that in order to do that, they had to admit it took a woman's body to bring them into this world. For them to be walking their talk, they had to admit to that. So that meant that they have to love their mom.

I believe that in the beginning of our world it was a goddess world. Now it's slowly turning—it went patriarchal—now it's slowly turning back to being a goddess world, I believe, because us women care, because we're natural nurturers, we care about our environment. We care about how our children will have water. We care about their health. We care because we love, because we brought them into the world. I hope that you will slowly begin to understand that more and more women that have been suppressed throughout the world—that this will stop, that we have equality. I have worked in the justice system. I know what's been happen-ing. I pray that more and more women will be stepping up and taking these beautiful jobs and empowering themselves.

18
PARENTING

When you're a mom, it's like you are in a world that you've never been in before. You have that feeling. Every day a new experience, being a mother. When you are a grandmother, you have been a mother so you kind of already know what a new life coming through is all about. When you're a great-grandma, it's enfolded again that you have an obligation to help those that are coming.

The kids wanted me to be over at the birth of that fourteenth grandchild. So, I was there. They were so glad I was there. I prayed for my granddaughter, and the nurses said it was so great that she never had pain, no shots. She had an all-natural birth. They said they hadn't seen that in a long, long time. What did it do to my heart? It made me feel good, because my teachings paid off.

One of the things you've got to be is attentive to the sound. You can hear your child. You immediately can feel if she is comfortable; you can immediately feel if she is worried; you immediately can feel if she is centered; you can feel if she is restless. Why is she restless? All of these instant things come to you as a mother. You are going to immediately know when the behavior has turned and it's not good for her. It'll immediately register as, "What's she's doing?" And you're always watchful if they're going to do something where they'll get hurt. You're always sensitive to that, but you don't say it. You're always aware because you're guarding, you're watching, you're listening to what is around your child.

You automatically do that. When she goes to school it's the same thing. Is she feeling good? You register that. Is she helping herself learn to get dressed, or do I need to help? All of that doesn't have to be verbal; you just know when to put your two hands out as a mother. You know that in order to give love, you hug. They recognize that momma loves me, she hugged me, yet she don't verbalize it, she just wilts in your arms. That's registering.

Your actions speak louder than words around children. They can tell whether you like 'em or not. Immediately—maybe first, second grade, around there—they know if they're loved. They know immediately what abuse is. If they got spanked, they know. If they got slapped, they know whether you love them behind all that. My kids, when they were younger, used to fight each other. I said, "Go out and cut yourself a switch." Well, they came in with the littlest twig you could get. And so I said, "When you're fighting, now I am going to show what hurts." And I would switch their legs. "See? That hurts. That's what you're doing to her. That's what he's doin' to her. That's what you're doin' to each other. Why? Why do you want to hurt like that?"

I never beat my kids, none of them. They can all say that. But I probably said something that hurt their feelings though, somewhere along. That's why I asked for forgiveness before I did this spiritual walk. I went to all of them and said, "Forgive me." Because there is no such thing as "parent school." We all make our mistakes as parents. Teach your child forgiveness. What is forgiveness? Ask 'em sometime, because someday you might have to ask them to forgive you. You might have said something, done something to hurt their feelings, so tell them what forgiveness is.

That's our job as parents, to teach our kids. What is love? Actions. Action for love is what you teach a kid. Use your actions. Hug. Kiss them on the cheek. Pat them. Or just say, "I love you." Many kids don't get that. They don't get those words, "I love you." Parents don't say it. All this abuse and roughness and cuss words. But to truly love your child is a great gift that you can give them, one of the *greatest* gifts you can give them. You don't have to have borne a child to love it. I love you, but you didn't come from me. It's a way you can show through behavior. And if it's your own child, always let them know: "Come here. I haven't hugged you today." Like my daughter that lives with me. We never go to bed at night without saying, "I love you. Goodnight. I love you." She always tells me, "I love you, Mother." I hear her and it is good, it is good.

I know that when I lie down, all is well when I go to sleep because I have that four-letter word: *love*. So simple. So simple. Your actions back that up. Once in a while I will go, "Let's go out to eat, because you're always cooking. It gives you a break." That shows her I love her. I have a dishwasher, but sometimes I am a dishwasher, when I can. Sometimes I can't stand there very long to get 'em done, and if I can't, she does 'em, but she doesn't grouch at me. That, to me, is love. But I do what I can. Like yesterday, I changed my bed by myself. I have always tried to do it by myself. Pull my mattress over—I have one of those electric pads so if I get cold, I can push a button and my back is nice and warm. I have an electric blanket over that, but I don't use it lately. So I made my bed all nice and clean; so I can do those things. I do my own laundry. I fold my own clothes. I make my lunch. If she's not there, she doesn't have to worry about Mom. She knows I have two hands, I can do it. It's good. It's called gratitude. She's grateful that I can do these things so that she can go visit her great-grandkids and not fuss about Mom, because Mom can still do it.

19
MARRIAGE

I am a licensed minister, so I marry people. I talk to them if I have to marry someone. I don't really like to get into that because I want them to know that getting married is going from being one to being two. I usually make them get a blanket so that when I marry them, I wrap them: "You are one. Remember that in all things. Don't go buying something that you don't talk over your partner with. Don't go spending some huge bunch of money and you haven't talked it over. You are a company. You need to be aware of all these. You're not just one person any more. It is a 'sharesies' kind of thing, and you've got to share. You've got to sit down and talk." I tell them, "Have conversation, even at the end of the day, even if it gets redundant: 'I did this today, and I did this. And this made me feel good, and I felt bad about that.' It's sharing in a good way because you're not one anymore, you're two." So, you have to do that. Learn to compromise. You are not going out and doing something and hiding it from somebody else, because that's being dishonest. I don't like the word *dishonesty* because that is lying to your partner in a subtle kind of way, but it's still untruthful. You got to learn to share. Share everything. Share your time. Share your love. Share everything you've got.

When my husband was alive and we lived in Crescent City, we'd find somebody—usually we would watch out for Indians hitchhiking on the highway—we picked them up, took them home, put them in my husband's pajamas. Washed their clothes. Fed them. Let them shower. Made them a big lunch. Got them a jug of water. Take 'em out three miles so that they can go on their way. They would stand there and look us over to see if we meant well or not. We'd do that. But I wouldn't do it by myself, pick somebody up. I always had my husband with me, and he'd say, "Pick 'em up." So there was two of us. But anyway, we did things like that. We had some who'd write to us once they got back home to Alaska or some state and thank us. They didn't need to do that. We already felt thankful in our heart. We are doing it. We done a lot of things like that.

20
INJUSTICE AND INEQUALITY

I worked in the justice system out of Del Norte County in Northern California for nearly twenty years, and I saw the injustice and inequality. I worked in the courtrooms. I saw the injustice, the imbalance, from the get-go when I started working in the courtroom. From that time on, I wanted to change it. I looked it up. I searched it out. Then, when us Grandmas came together, I talked to them about it, and some of them knew and some of them didn't.

In 1493 Pope Alexander VI of the Vatican wrote an edict, a papal bull, which in essence said for the powers to go around the world and to search out the land. If they were occupied and if they were pagan and heathen, to kill them—*pagan* and *heathen* meaning they weren't Roman Catholic—to kill them and take the land. We all know what Columbus did at the East Coast at that time. He met with the Six Nations there, and he saw this land was occupied and they were pagan and heathen, meaning they were not Catholic people. When he left, then came the guns and the Trail of Tears that came across this United States, killing our First Nation people and wiping out some tribes completely.

I was swarmed in Australia when I talked about it because they know what's happening. New Zealand knows what's happened. I said many, many, many, many times—I have been on microphones, televisions, and everything. I would like to have the audience with the new Pope because they said Pope John Paul had written a letter denouncing this papal bull. I said, "Then I would like to see that letter." "Pope John Paul is gone." "Well, where is the letter?" Nobody knows. So now Pope Francis, I feel, has got that kind of charisma that you can sit down and he would lend you his ear in a calm, nice way. I think he has got that type of character that he would listen to what I am saying. So, I have been wanting to meet the Pope.

Us 13 International Grandmas went to the Vatican to meet with Pope John Paul about this papal bull. We were there in the front of the Sistine Chapel; he had addressed the people there every Wednesday. They came in by the thousands in busloads, and he would address them there. We wrote to him but we never got a response to our letter, so we went there, all of us. We laid down our altar, and we put our sacred things on it. The first thing we knew, here come a cop and said we were desecrating this ground: "This land and this country is for prayer." Then here come another one saying the same thing, "We're going to put you in jail if you don't clean this up. You have no right." Then here come a big tall cop—all of this is in our movie—and here come a tall guy, officer, and he settled the other two down a little bit. Anyway, here come one of our ladies that bought us a permit to be there. But we didn't get to see Pope John Paul because he'd taken off for Australia.

I still would like to meet with Pope Francis because I think he would have an ear to understand the injustice that has happened. Nobody ever asked what happened to the Aboriginal and indigenous people all over the world. They were killed all over the world, and this is the same with my people here. So, I would like to meet with Pope Francis to see if he could rescind that edict. It's been over five hundred years, and there's nobody alive today that had anything to do with that. Why not rescind it. I pray that Pope Francis believes in equality and justice, and I think he would listen and try to do something about it. I have a dream, and that's one of them that maybe would get his ear, because he seems like he's got the type of charisma, you know, of listening and having compassion for elders and children. I think he would listen.

I hope that maybe I get that opportunity—that two or three of us International Grandmas could go and be with him, to have this thing done away with. I don't care for myself, but I would like to see the equality and justice for all of those that are behind me, my fifth-generation little kids. I would like to see that equality, for them to have that. I think that any grandparent should want that for their kids and for the First Nation people. I would also like to see the state of Oregon take Columbus Day and make October 12 declared First Nation Day. Join me. I would love to see that. The only reason why I celebrate October 12 is because I got only one son left, Keith, and his birthday is October 12. That's the only reason why I celebrate it. Think about it, and get ahold of me. Let's get rolling on it, and let's get it changed, or let's get it on the map. I really thank you.

I am who I am, and I am very proud that I walk. My parents aren't here today. They're gone, and all my brothers and sisters are gone, but that's who I am. I am a First Nation woman, and I really am proud of who I am. Especially when I am in my regalia. That's totally who I am. I am proud to be that. I am glad that there are no more signs around the cities where I grew up in Lincoln County, that dogs and Indians are not allowed. I am glad we don't see those signs anymore. I am proud to be a First Nation woman.

My dad's last name was Baker, that's why I use Agnes Baker-Pilgrim, in honor and respect to my dad and to honor my parents, because I love them. I still love them even though they're over there. They've taught me a lot, and I am so proud of all the things that they taught me when I was a kid: how to survive on this earth, and about how sacred everything was. I am really proud to be this First Nation woman and to have all my children. They are grandparents, and a couple of them are great-grandparents now. I am proud that I walk in front of them, that I can leave a wonderful legacy to them. So teach your kids kindness and forgiveness, because you make mistakes, too. I hope that you listen and do that. Above all, love your children even before they come out of the amnio sac—you love them. That's why you have them. Treat them with love. Love is all there is, is what I teach. I thank you again for listening.

When I went down in the south, all the colored people were in the back of the bus. My skin was as dark as theirs, but they took me for a light-skinned black woman. So I was a colored person—back of the bus. I had a card stating who I was, and I showed the driver. "No argument, I am just showing you. Here it is. This is who I am." So he let me sit wherever I wanted to sit. But I was duking it out with people even just being Indian and, that was tough. Calling me a *squaw* is like a red flag in front of a bull. Man, I got in a lot of fights. I even got a busted nose from that. But anyway, I was always sticking up for people—I didn't like two people on one person.

One time my husband and I was goin' to Portland. He turned off the Broadway Bridge and was going along Second Street. There was two white women beatin' up this Indian woman. "Stop the car!" I told him. Out I went. I duked one over clear into the street and got the other one, and I said, "We're going to even this up a little bit." I got them going off down the street, and I picked up that Indian lady and took her down to where she wanted to go. I always was like that for somebody getting abused and it wasn't a fair thing. I always stood up for them. I don't care who it was or how big they were. It didn't matter. I get a lot of respect now, but there is still that idea of "I am not up here." I should be up here, but I am not. I placed me "up here," but the whole country doesn't place me there, even with the status I have as an International Grandmother. I don't care what happens with this papal bull, but I do care because of all my children that would be here to go through with it, because I have watched the injustice in the courtroom, because I am looked down on. Our native people are looked down on. I have been in the courtrooms working and telling the judge and the jurors that that Indian boy up there, if he doesn't look at you, don't pronounce him guilty, because he has been taught not to look at people when he talks to them. So, don't say he's guilty. I've done that.

Young babies have been taken away from mothers right there in Del Norte County. They got a Samoan, take him to emergency. The doctors see the blue marks on his body and said the mother had been abusing him. They just ripped the baby from her hands and put it in a safe home. I said, "None of this is right." What did I do? I went to the hospital and got all the staff together and told them: that is birthmarks. People of color have this—all of mine do. I went to the welfare and told them. I went to the police department and educated them on this. Babies of color have these markings, which some kids outgrow—it goes away. Some it doesn't. But I said, "It is there, so you have to know and realize that." I fought for that with the court system.

So there's an injustice because you got this color and you got the name of Indian. I don't like that word. I like *First Nation*. I am a First Nation woman, and I would like to see that name put on every Indian person's ID. *First Nation*. We are First Nation people. Right now I am on sacred ground. I speak here in the United States, anywhere in the United States, and it's sacred ground. I always say that I am on sacred ground. I am on native land. That's the respect I give to Mother Earth. So I am fighting all the time for equality and justice, and I think that Pope Francis would listen. I really do.

21
EVERYBODY HAS A GIFT

Everybody, from the time they were little, we're given a gift: of life, for one thing, and second thing was this thinkin' thing. But we all got gifts. I don't believe that there's anybody that's ever told me that they don't have any, 'cause they all got something. I got a lot of them. I bead. I make clothes. I have done a lot of stuff. I was a musician. I could play violin, piano, plucked a banjo, guitar. I sang all over the country. I was a race driver. I was a boxer. I did a lot of things.

Think about it. This is why my own people, at the end of the day, they didn't have televisions and radios and things to entertain them. When the sun went down, they felt good of their accomplishment. There's another fifty-cent word: *accomplishment.* By the time you go to bed, what have you accomplished? You're not put here just to take up space. We're all supposed to be doers of some sort. You do this, do that, when you get that done you do something else. You know, it's activity. You got to be active in order to be able to do things.

To me, if I walk in truth, if I am true to me, then I am true to you, and you and you. That's the way I run my life. I don't care if it is even working a crossword puzzle. I don't like to look at the crossword book and look at the answers and say I did it. That's how honest I am to me, because this thinkin' thing has to be right. I believe this thing is the most powerful thing you've got, and how you run it is how long you stay on this planet, because this thing has to tell your body, "I want to live a long time."

He gave us this thinkin' thing and put it on top of our body to run the rest of it. That's why, when people get so depressed and they go on and on telling me why they are depressed, and they go along with their selves so far down, that's why I say, "Are you through?" "Yes" "May I ask you something? Who is running your brain? Because your brain got you down there, and your brain, if you run it right, can get you back out and get you back up in the sunshine belt." We owe it to this thinkin' thing to get us up in the sunshine belt. That's where health is. That's where love is. That's where caring is, and sharing, and compassion, all this stuff. Just like I told my kids, "I can't give it to you kids. You got to create it in your own self; of kindness, forgiveness, all of that, you have got to do your own. If you want kindness with somebody, then you better have it in there. If you want love, you better have it in there. And I am not talking about eagle love. If you want compassion and joy and smiles and laughter, it is your job. Dad can't give it to you. Grandma, Grandpa, none of us can give it to you. You got to create it."

Even though I grew up where signs said "No dogs and Indians allowed," it didn't make me bitter. Didn't make me hate the white race. It is something that I don't—I don't use the word *hate*. I don't use it literally, because I think that you can't serve two Gods. The devil is one, and my beloved Creator is the other. So, you can't serve this one over here if you are going to serve this one over here. You put up a barrier before your prayer will go out, it will not go through. And so I say you can't serve two Gods. If something evil comes up, the Creator will take care of it. I know my limits. I don't have to deal with it. I know my perimeters. I can put the word out there, and if they don't accept it, is it my fault? I can't change you. If I put all these words here today and if you accept some of them, that's fine. If you don't accept all of them, that's fine, too. Can I change that? No way in heaven. Creator told me I do not sit in judgment of you.

So I don't sit in judgment of people's choices of how they live their life. I am not God. There is only one God, and I am not it. I don't sit and criticize, and I don't put people down—nobody, whether you're black, striped, or polka dots. I can't change nobody but myself. I can't change my kids. They're all grown up. You can lead a horse to water. Can you make him drink? Not unless he wants to. I could see this, you could see this, but I see something you don't see and you see something I don't see, right? We all have a right to that opinion verbally, or follow up what we see with actions. Another thing I always tell my kids, don't ever forget that you've got a choice, to think of the payoff. If there's an action, there's a reaction. What you're doing, what's the reaction of it? Question yourself. "Should I do this or should I not do this?" If it comes to that question, then you better figure out what is the lesser of two evils.

Anybody could do what I been doin', and that is to help people to think different. If I can think different in a better way—just like I teach people that the cheapest thing we got is laughter. Do you know that is one of our cheapest medicines? Laughter. Because when you're laughing, you are up in the sunshine belt, as I say, and your body heals, and your mind comes along. Laughter. Lightness of spirit. If you can find something to laugh about—you have a tickle button, you know—use it once in a while, because that makes you feel better about yourself. It lightens your spirit and gives you a different outlook, even about yourself, when you can find something to laugh at. I always say, that's our cheapest medicine that we got.

There's so much simplicity of life that a lot of people don't even think about. The simplicity of, in the morning, taking a glass of water and saying, "Thank you for my life" kind of simple. Don't even have to be verbalized. You just run through this thing and say, "Bless you for my life." I do that ritualistically every day for over five years now. God is good, and all life that He's given us. Laughter, of all things—you owe it to yourself, your life, your daily life, to laugh. When you're laughing, your immune system is up in the sunshine belt. Your body heals, and your mind comes along. So give it a good blast of *a ha ha ha ha* at least once a day. Everybody has a humor button, so use it. Laughter is lightening your spirit, and I pray that you can do that.

Don't be so doom and gloom. I can't live around people that are gloom and doom because I can't change nobody but myself. So, if you're down and you're gloom and doom, your brain has put you in there. If you want some sunshine, you better get your brain workin' right and bring it back up in the sunshine belt. That's your job. Nobody can give it to you. Mom, Dad, Grandma, Grandpa can't give you the sunshine belt. That's your own inside work. I pray that you can lighten your brain up and give yourself a good laugh at least once a day as good medicine. It is good medicine, so try it out. Lighten your load. Think about it. Teach it to your kids. Have fun with them. Laughter is a great thing in all life, being a little tiny baby or anybody.

I just had the fourteenth child of my fifth generation. Already those little kids are smiling. So, they got it inside, and they already know that they can smile. Pretty soon, when they get a little bigger, I know they're going to add laughter to that.

You have an obligation to yourself. If you want wellness, if you want healthiness in your mind and your body, then you owe your body a good laugh at least once a day. So, get up in the sunshine belt. Your immune system is more in a healthy spot, and your body heals and your mind comes along. So give yourself the cheapest medicine we got, and that's laughter.

22
RECONNECTING

My First Nation people that have been raised in an asphalt jungle, that are not on the reservation, they don't know their own people's walk. It's scary to know that here you are, a First Nation person, but you don't know what it's like to be part of your tribe because you've been raised in the city. When we came together in New York, you know, I had people say, "We're in the city. How do we pray about plants? We don't have any of those here in the city." I said, "But you could pray that somewhere somebody that has that knowledge could take care of these plants." And it is happening; more and more people are growing things.

When I was in Italy, on the terraces people are growing different types of plants up on their balconies, way up high. Some of it is for medicine. Some of it is for spices. If you learned, you could grow these things. My Grandma Flordemayo says that anybody could get these seeds and grow your medicines. How to prepare them is something you have to learn. So, everybody has an opportunity to learn about plant life, whether it is a regular garden, whether it is medicine plants, or whether it is a flower. The knowledge is out there if they want to search and find it.

You know, with me, I grew up with gardens. With everything, my father would go gather medicines. I wish I could remember some of the things that he made for us kids, because we were way out in the country, miles from doctors. So we had to have something quick if we were getting sick. How to make a sweat—he'd make stuff up and make us drink it. Cover us with blankets so we could sweat it out. If we had a sore that wouldn't heal, he would mix up stuff and put a poultice over it and draw it out. Some people got boils that he'd mix up stuff for them and put some cloth over them and put that packed stuff on it and put a cloth over it and draw that stuff out. I wish I could remember what he used, but I was little and never thought of those things. That type of knowledge is out there for anybody.

If you want to help yourself, whatever the sickness you have, there's something out there that you could take. But it's up to you to kind of nose around, search around to find out where it's at. Can you grow it? Is the climate okay here in Oregon to grow it? You have to find out all these things about its habitat, what is good for us. We got to think beyond our nose about a lot of these things that we want to understand. The knowledge is out there. If you want to study about medicine plants and you have that calling, you'll find places for any of it anywhere. Where the medicines are, how to grow them, what they're for; it is all out there anywhere you go. If you're curious enough, most all the medicines are in some sort of an encyclopedia or they're registered in some book of some kind.

I don't care if it's heart problems, cancer, or whatever. There's medicines for all of this. So, you could search it out. There's all kinds of different places, and different countries have different wordings, but the knowledge is there. In any country anybody wants to travel to, they have the knowledge now. You could go anywhere. If I go to Africa, if they have yellow fever, they have some medicines for me. Or I could get it prior here before I go. Any sickness that we have, there is some sort—I always say there's a plant for that cure. That knowledge is stuck somewhere. I believe that science has not searched deep enough to find the cure for cancer, but I believe that there is a cure upon this planet for all—any kind of disease, rash, or anything we get for our body, a cure is on this planet.

Every place I've been in the world, Creator has done beautiful work of letting medicine plants grow in different parts of the country, that taught people from way back there where to go to get them and how to use them. We even thanked deer because humans watched what the deer ate, and if the deer would eat certain things, then we could eat it. So, the deer helped us a lot, I guess, in the First Nation people, to teach us what was good for us and what we could eat. So, we learned from the animal kingdom.

I had to pray for my Grandma in South America because down there where she was gathering all of her medicines, they cut all the trees down. Her medicine plants were growing below the trees and she was frightened. Even the man that owned that property was getting her medicine, so I told her, "You go tell him what he's done. Maybe he will have some other land where you can gather your plants underneath them trees that he hasn't sold." So she was supposed to have done that. There's medicine plants all over the world. It is like our Grandma in Africa—some of the plants that they use for medicine she cannot use anymore, but one of our other Grandmas got that plant, and she is raising it and using it.

I know there are plants in different countries all over the world. Even when I was in Katmandu they told us of different plants that came from over there in Nepal. I know the Creator has been good to us to see that these medicines were in different places all over on the planet and for us to be aware of them to use. I believe that every disease that us humans can get, there's a remedy out there, even to cancer. They just haven't found it. I hope that the scientists that are still searching and looking will find it so that they will save lives. That's important to me, to be able to have people not get cancer. I have had cancer. I have had radical mastectomies. I have had a foot and a half of my colon taken out. I've been to hell and back with pain. I've had chemo and radiation for months and months and months. I nearly lost my hair. It used to be thick, but now it just got a little bit to cover my head. But I don't complain and holler about it because I got some up there. And I am alive, and I've been a survivor since

1982 because I think I've got miles to go yet and I got things to do and people to help, people to love, people to teach.

People have asked me, "You've been all over the world, Grandma. What's your favorite place?" And I said, "You know, wherever my feet put me down, I am home, because that's family." Stop being biased and prejudiced about the color of somebody's skin. We're all from the same Creator, but there's many different paths to the Creator. He is known by many, many names. I choose to call Him the Great Spirit, the Creator, my beloved Creator. He is in my heart every morning, all through the day. I give thanks just for being, just for being able to take this little spot here today. I am grateful to be alive and to be able to help in any way I can. Like our pow wows. People say "Why pow wows?" It's the coming together in friendship and love, and reacquainting one another, and meeting old friends. It's coming together and standing tall, being who we are.

When I am in my regalia, that's exactly who I am. I feel proud to be in my buckskins and be this Native, this First Nation person that I am. I said, "I pray to God that the old chiefs that are in my background smile at me on my walk. Especially when I'm in my regalia and come together with all my family. I am one mother in our tribe of Siletz, Oregon, that is walkin' tall because all my kids come and they are all dressed down. They're chemical-free, no tobacco, no pills, no alcohol. Man, I am proud. I am walkin' ten foot tall with them so that they, too, will leave a good legacy for their children when they go to the Star Nation.

I feel like I am doing my job in a good way, without even words. It's how I conduct my life day by day. I feel like I live in a glass house, which is okay. I don't care because I am doin' my best to say and to do. My life is an open book, and so to have the pow wows and stuff that come up, it is an honor to all of us because that's who we are, First Nation people. I would like to get everybody to support me here in Oregon to have October 12—that's my son Keith's birthday, is the only reason why I celebrate October 12—to take Columbus Day and make it into First Nation Day. Washington State has done it. Why can't we?

Close around the 18th of November we honor coming back into a recognized tribe. They have that at Chinook Winds upstairs, and it's a huge floor up there where we all come to be happy because we are a recognized tribe. The Menominees were first. After the termination of the Menominees tribe was first, we were second. All those years, twenty-something years of being a no-nation person, I felt like a drifter on the river. I didn't belong here. I didn't belong here, just driftin' along. So when we come back as a recognized tribe, man, I tell you, I cried. I cried for days of gratitude. How it made me feel is like having a puzzle and you couldn't find one piece to finish. It doesn't feel like it's done. That's the way I felt. But when we came back as recognized people, I felt like peace was found in my heart. I felt wholeness. I felt good. I felt happy. I was crying because I didn't belong to any place all those years. It was a god-awful feeling to me.

When we were restored, I thought how great it is to be able to fit and belong. Thirty-six years; it is a good feeling to talk about it now, to feel whole and that you fit and you belong. The gratitude I have for all of those, even my brothers. I never did want to be on a tribal council because I was a spiritual person and I thought, god, I wear an arrow shirt every day as it is, let alone be in there and be cussed out, cussed up, and cussed down. Damned-if-you-do and damned-if-you-don't position. So I never wanted to be on tribal council. My place is prayer. My spiritual place is to uphold our tribal council and to pray for it. It's a bumpy road for them, too. It's hard. It's hard, that political fuel, because you get lied to all the time about something from some corner of the world, and it's a hard position. You have to be tough, and you have to be congenial when you don't feel like it. I come into all our tribal council, those who have gone. Even when we were terminated we kept our tribal council, thank God. So when we gave testimony, we gave testimony that we stayed with our tribal songs all the time and kept it going. I am proud of those that

were those far-seers, to see how great that would mean when we
gave testimony, that they saw to it, that they still carried on even
without the recognition. But I commend them for the freedom I
feel right now talking about it, and the feeling of belonging, that
I fit and belong. That's okay.

Ashland is a threshold of people coming in from California.
You don't see nothing of my people. I think to honor them, this
alder tree could do it. Not only those that's goin' on, but our
Native students that are going to come to Southern Oregon
University, they need something here to show them that there's
been Native people here on this land. So there is now a spirit pole
in Ashland that came through an attorney, Matthew Haines. He
had, below this alder tree, a deck built. He said he'd like to see if
he could get the tree out. We had to meet with the city council
to get that tree out. The carver, Russell Beebe, and I went before
the Ashland City Council to tell them what we were going to do
with that tree. It was an alder tree. Matthew wanted the carver to
carve me on that tree, and we could plant it further up the hill.

I came over there for the city council, and I told them that,
you know, the alder tree is not like hardwood trees. I said, "If
along comes some snow or something, heavy wind, somebody
could get hurt." They have this cemented place below the tree,
and it has chairs where people can sit out there. I said, "It doesn't
have a lifespan like an oak or a sturdier tree, so it needs to come
out. And he is only going to move it about thirty-five feet up
the hill there." So, I talked to the city council about it, and they
agreed to let the tree come out. Then the carver, Russell Beebe,
even went around it with fire, and we talked to that tree about
what we were going to do with it, that it is going to be made into
perpetuity. "We are going to carve on you, we're going to make
you beautiful. You'll live forever, but we're going to move you up
here." We talked to it like a human being.

Russell, an Ojibway man, got the tree and took it to his property and tied it up between two other trees. He built a scaffold,
and he began to carve me on that tree. I took over some of my

necklaces and stuff so he could carve them, and a design of my basket cap that he took and put on my head that he could carve. It was carved on this alder tree. So Russell did carve it with all the animals on it. I told some of the history teachers that this is a family, because they put a baby in a papoose basket behind me. On the other side of the tree was a Shasta man holding a little child. Then all of the animals—the deer, the elk, the cougar, the eagle, the snake—all these animals were carved on this tree around us.

Well, after it was in place, it begin to crack and it begin to mold, and Russell had to crawl up and down and correct everything. So then Matthew and I decided maybe we better find an inside place on campus for it. So we walked all around, and we got to the library. We were in the foyer and we were looking around. He said we could put it here, and I said oh no, we don't want it in the foyer because people will be carving it and putting their names on it. I said, "I don't want it out there. This is a sacred thing to me. I am speaking for the tree, so we can't have it there." So we looked around, and we found a room next to the foyer in front of a window that you could see the tree from the window. So that's where it is at this time, is inside. Russell carved eight-foot benches for people to go and meditate or to have any type of classes there; they would have room. He's made some beautiful benches. He's given one to me that had a beautiful eagle on it and its feathers clear down to the floor, intricately carved, his big claws down underneath that. He gave me one with a big salmon on it for the foyer of our museum for our tribe. So he has carved these big eight-foot benches around the spirit pole, and I thought that way people could come and pray, or you could have some sort of a program here about the tree where people could come and sit quietly or whatever. So that's where it is at, inside the library. It is there yet today.

Before that happened, Mathew found Jack Langford, who is a bronze sculptor. Jack needed a job, so Matthew got him at a crucial time to pay for Jack to do the spirit pole in bronze. When it was time for us to go over there and to mount it, I told city council,

"You'll have to shut down the street. I don't want anybody, especially children, getting hurt." "No. We can't." I said, "What's sixty minutes compared to 250 or 550 years? Every one of you is sittin' on tribal ground right here today. This was our people's land." And I said, "I, too, am standing here talking to you on native ground." I described why we were putting that bronze tree there, in honor to Native students at Southern Oregon University. Also, to remember the ancient ones of the land would be this tree, to stand in perpetuity in honor of the First Nation people. So they closed the street; they did that for us when we put the bronze cast of the spirit pole up. So we put it up there where the original spirit pole was before we moved it to the campus.

We had singers to come and people to speak, and Danny Wahpepah of the Red Earth Descendants was there with the drum, and my adopted son David West was there—he has been a professor here at the university—and Brent Florendo, a Native American studies teacher at Southern Oregon University. All of the Native people that were here came. We named the sculpture "We Are Here," and we are here. And I did it not for me, but in honor of those in my background who did it in this land, to give them that recognition, to let people know you're standing on native ground. They would've still been here, but they were driven out in 1956, every one of them. Yet they thought the Creator gave them this land just for them because they'd lived here for 22,000 years.

I felt very honored to work with Matthew Haines and Russell Beebe, and it was a great honor to be able to do this for our people, for the Old Ones. That's why I wanted it—for them to be recognized in my background. It was a good feeling. The artist's name and my name are there to this day. So there it stands, the carving in bronze. I feel very honored that, when I go to the Star Nation, that there will be that spirit pole because, as I say, Ashland is a threshold and there is nothing Native out there. Now we have the bronze that will show there were residents of First Nation people there. I feel very good to have it standing there. It is still a good feeling to see it as I go by.

We're poor people money-wise but rich in many ways. If I lie or if I do things that are opposite of what I am talking, then it is not true. So, I better watch out what I am doin' because of this on my chin—that's *111*. And the same way with Arvol Looking Horse. He's in a position, and he's looked up to by all our people, from the little ones up to the elders, and you better walk your talk or you're going to carry that pipe and wear it around you. How the Creator has burdened him, too, with the carrying of the pipe. That's a man's job. You can feel the strength in Arvol Looking Horse because he is given that position. When you carry, you better by-god be doing the right thing and saying the right words, because we all know the karma. Like me, I got this, I know the karma. That means that when you're just quietly by yourself, is this thinkin' thing saying the good stuff? 'Cause the pipe could pick it up. When you're a pipe carrier, you got to be careful what you're doing, what you're saying, and how you're doing it. It comes some way from the spirit world.

A long time ago I was down out of Rohnerville with the Lincoln family in California at Sundance. They had me come to bless the inside of the place where they're fasting. At Coyote Valley they had me to bless their sweat lodge. They had me to bless the hole where they were gonna put the cottonwood tree. The cottonwood tree is symbolic of all tribal people. They had me go down when they cut the tree. All the young girls, the virgins, go, and they touch the tree first, then they allowed me to come. So from the get-go we blessed the cottonwood tree, and they put it on this great big long trailer. When they put it on the big trailer to haul it up—because it's not to touch the ground—I was the first car behind that tree. Then when they brought it up, I went out to the hole that they'd dug, and I had to drop some medicine down in there before they put the tree in. When the tree is up, then I have to go all around under the arbor and bless it and do all of those things. So they had been watching my life or I wouldn't have been asked to do that.

I had made prayer bundles to put around the tree, so my prayer bundles was the first to go up, which is the red and yellow and black and white. The sky is the blue one, the red is the person, and the green at the bottom is for the earth. They're on a string with all these balls, and it went around the top of the tree. Then everybody brings theirs to put up on the tree. When they were done, it was the most beautiful Sundance tree I ever saw, with all of the flags representative of people all over the country. It was just amazing.

They handed me the pipe four times. I was astounded that the pipe came to me four times because I am not raised with the pipe, but the honor being that they gave me that because they knew of my walk, that I was worthy to be able to touch the pipe. My daughter Nadine was with me. She was dancing on the side, and she handed me that pipe, and I was awestruck—four times.

Another time, we were back at our first gathering in South Dakota with our Grandma Beatrice Long Visitor Holy Dance when their tree was taken down, and I was involved with all of that. She honored me to have them take me down there to be with the virgins to bless that tree, too. They have a huge arbor with shade, and I went all around the arbor. They got limbs and things up there that they cover it with so you can get in the shade. All around the arbor, I blessed it. I went inside where they were fasting and blessed the people that were going to be out there with buffalo skulls tied to their chest, and they pull the buffalo skulls around. They pull until it rips the skin. I was behind them when they pulled the skulls around them.

My Grandma Beatrice's son was the first to pull three skulls behind him, and I was behind him, and the dust was flying, and they were pushing me in a wheelchair behind him. That's what he wanted. Then, when the skulls broke loose—he was a diabetic— well, I am sitting over there, and Spirit told me to go over there and put my hands over those torn places of his flesh and to pray. I said, "I can't do that. You tell somebody else." It came again: "You go over there and put your hands—you don't have to touch his body, just cup your hands over those sore places and pray." "Oh, all right." So I went over there. I told him, "Spirit told me to come over here, that you were diabetic, and I can cup my hands over your sores here so you won't get infection." So I stood there and did that. Now, he's alive yet today, and he could tell you this. I did pray as the Creator told me to do it, so I cupped my hands over those places where he is bleeding so he wouldn't get infection, and he didn't.

It's amazing how Creator bosses me around. Sometimes I have to argue with Him, but I still do it. He's got a cauliflower ear because I am always badgering Him about stuff. But there are things like that Spirit has told me I had to do. I don't know if He's ever come to you like that, if something fly out of your mouth and you say, well, I never thought of that until just now. So much stuff comes to me sometimes. I always have a pen and piece of paper by my bed because some things come that I think, I better remember this one, and I will write it down. Then there's a name that comes sometimes that Spirit tells me I'd better call. So, I will write that name down so I won't forget. Sometimes there is a sentence that I am supposed to remember to include somewhere, not knowing where that somewhere is. I write it down, but it always comes where I am supposed to put it. Little things like that gets me overwhelmed sometimes.

The Creator can open these doors. Like when He called me to do the spiritual path and I said, "No. I can't do it. I am not worthy. Give it to somebody else." Well, it kept coming, and it kept coming. One day, one of my friends who is a psychologist out of Arcata, California—Dr. Royal Alsup—he said, "When are you going to quit fighting this and do it?" I said, "Well, I guess I could do it today." And when I said that, it was like a big load went off my back. So I began the walk, and I listened to the Creator.

I don't know whether you get any responses from the beloved Creator. I always ask people, and sometimes something pops out of your mouth and you say, "Gee, I wonder where that came from." Well, it's maybe the ancient ones behind you, or maybe it's the Creator. So I don't worry about it. I don't fuss about it. When it comes like that, it was meant to be for me to do or act or to say. So I always nudge the Creator, and I say, "Blessed Creator, you must have a cauliflower ear because I am nothing without You, so I am always thumping it." Always give thanks just for being. Every day when I wake up in the morning, "Bless you. I got another day." Because there's been times in my life when I was in so much pain that I begged to die. "Take me. Take me. I've had it. I can't stand no more." But there again, He held me up and stood me up.

So here I am, still walking on this path on Mother Earth. I better be careful what I am doing, because I got one foot on this earth and one in the other world. Creator has used me for so many years now—not just for my family but for others that have two ears, one mouth—that I have teached them this and then they could teach somebody else. Because I always speak truth. Everything you are reading here today is truth. I walk that way. I walk my path in integrity from the very depth of my heart every day, the best I can, with the love I have of the Creator. I don't know what it means to you, but He is in my life and in my heart and in my mind. You can pray whether you're sittin' down by the river or in your car or sittin' on the john. The Creator can hear you because He has created all of us. I don't go anywhere without giving thanks for the Creator being with me. I always say if your sky pilot don't work, mine does. I will loan it to ya, because it always helps me.

He's with me at all times. I am never alone. I feel good about that. Someday I'll be able to face the Creator when I go the Star Nation, and I can sit there and tell Him, "Thank you for being in my life and in my heart and with me every day, and to keep me on this earth." And He says "Use me." He put me on the spiritual path, so I know I am not done yet. I just keep on keepin' on and thankin' Him every day for my life. I thank Him for the words that He always gives, to be able to leave some of these things that I have experienced and some of these words that I have to leave behind, not just to the women but to the men, too, and for all of us to be able to carry on in a good way as you walk your life. You're walking in front of your family; you're walking in front of the public. They watch you like they watched me for four and a half years, my walk here in Southern Oregon, before my name come up to go and be one of the 13 International Grandmas.

They had watched my walk. It was like living in a glass house. I still live in a glass house, so I watch what I do. I have control over my behavior. Do you? If you don't, why not? You are not runnin' your head right if you're not. If you're abusing your body, your head's doin' it. Nobody is tying you up and pouring this stuff down there and making you take it. Take charge of your life. It's your job. That life that the Creator gave us is your responsibility to take care of it with gratitude and love, because the Creator gave it to us. So, I hope I have said something to encourage you and strengthen you, to make you feel good about who you are just for takin' up this little spot on Mother Earth's face. It's a thing that we all need to give thanks for, everybody.

The privileges that we have are great and many. Use them wisely for your life and for your longevity. Don't be abusing yourself, because it's a gift given to us. And to give thanks to Momma because it took her body to bring you into this world. I do. I always thank my mom and everybody in my background. It took all those Old Ones to make who I am, so I am grateful that it took all of them. I pray I am walkin' my talk in front of them. I know they help me, so they wouldn't be helping me if I wasn't doin' the right thing. You think about all of the Old Ones that it took to make you, and give thanks to them—Grandma's mom, Grandpa's mom, Grandpa and Grandma's moms, all the way back to your family's beginning—give thanks for all those lives that are inside of you. Learn to be grateful for just one day at a time, that's all we can do. I pray when you get up in the morning that you can fill it with all the good things. Think about what you're doin' every day. Is it benefitting you? Is it helping you? So, I thank you for listening. Bless you for another day.